Gathering the Artists:

What the Bible Says About God, Art, and Creativity

By Michael Galloway

© 2020 by Michael Galloway. All rights reserved.

ISBN-13: 978-1-67803-681-2

No part of this book may be reproduced, stored in a retrieval system, or transmitted by any means, electronic, mechanical, photocopying, recording or otherwise without written permission from the author.

www.michaelgalloway.net

Unless otherwise noted, all Scripture verses are taken from the King James Version.

Contents

The First Creator   7
The Artisans of the Tabernacle   11
The Temple Builders   17
The Writers   29
The Actors, Sculptors, and Dancers   37
The Musicians   45
The Image Makers   53
The Idol Makers   61
The Critics   69
The Great Mystery Writer   79

"Art is a reflection of God's creativity, an evidence that we are made in the image of God."—Francis Schaeffer

- 1 -

The First Creator

"The heavens declare the glory of God; and the firmament sheweth his handywork." − Psalm 19:1

When you think of God's characteristics, what comes to mind? Do words such as loving, patient, and forgiving make the list? How about eternal, unchanging, and lawgiving? Or do none of these words fit? Perhaps a different approach is in order. What about words such as architect, author, or composer? Regardless of the list, one word is often missing—creative.

Despite God often being described as the Creator, creative does not seem to be a common description that accompanies it. If creativity is even considered, it is often in terms of functionality rather than creation for the joy of it. According to Webster's Dictionary, some of the definitions of the word "create" include "to bring into existence" or to "design" or to "produce through imaginative skill." The words "skill" and "design" imply a purposeful and thought-out act on the part of the creator and the translation of a vision of the mind into a tangible form that others can appreciate. By extension, the word "creative" is defined as being "marked by the ability or power to create" or "given to creating". Usually the implication is artistic, or at least involves the generation of something original.

In Genesis 1:1 it states that "in the beginning God created the heaven and the earth." It is easy to rush by this well-known verse without thinking through what it actually means. If you stop to think for a moment about the amount of stars in the universe and the number of planets that may revolve around them, the numbers are bewildering. As of the writing of this book, some scientists estimate there are over one septillion stars in the observable universe. There are also over 4,000 known exoplanets, or planets orbiting around stars besides our sun, and more are being discovered all the time. One look at our own local Solar System shows an amazing variation from planet to planet in size, geology, and characteristics. From moonless Mercury to the gas giants to the tiny world of Pluto (with five moons of its own), there are endless sources of fascination. There are also exploratory missions ongoing and being planned with the hopes of gaining new understanding or perhaps colonizing these worlds.

The verses that follow then go into high-level detail about God's creation process for the earth, the heavens, seas, land, grass, trees, the sun, the moon, the stars, sea life, birds, land animals, and finally man. Although the summary is short and swift, stop and think about each item for a minute. Whole fields of science and mathematics have originated from the study of these objects and their related systems—from biology to astronomy to oceanography to medicine for example.

The Bible then takes it a step further. Not only does it state that God created man, but that man is made in God's image (Genesis 1:27) and that He "formed man of the dust of the ground, and breathed into his nostrils the breath of life; and man became a living soul." (Genesis 2:7) In essence, a distinction is made here between mankind and the other physical objects that have been created. This idea is also mentioned in a similar context in Isaiah 42:5, where it states that God "giveth breath unto the people upon it, and spirit to them that walk therein" (referring to those that walk upon the earth).

Building upon this, God declares He is also a creator of nations. In Isaiah 43:1 it states, "O Jacob, and He that formed thee, O Israel, Fear not: for I have redeemed thee, I have called thee by thy name; thou art Mine." Additionally, in Isaiah 43:15 it states, "I am the Lord, your Holy One, the creator of Israel, your King." This is a concept that appears several times in Scripture as we will see in later chapters.

Scripture does not stop there and explicitly states that Jesus is the one by whom the world was created and it is through Him that it holds together. Consider John 1:1 – 3 which reads, "In the beginning was the Word, and the Word was with God, and the Word was God. The same was in the beginning with God. All things were made by Him; and without Him was not any thing made that was made." In

Ephesians 3:9 it also states that God created "all things by Jesus Christ" and in Colossians 1:16 – 17, Paul wrote about Jesus, "For by Him were all things created, that are in heaven, and that are in earth, visible and invisible, whether they be thrones, or dominions, or principalities, or powers: all things were created by Him, and for Him: and He is before all things, and by Him all things consist."

Thinking through the complexity of all these systems and their interactions with one another, both visible and invisible, it does not take long for it to become overwhelming. The complexity also seems to have endless depth. As it says in Ecclesiastes 3:11, "He hath made every thing beautiful in His time: also He hath set the world in their heart, so that no man can find out the work that God maketh from the beginning to the end." Or, as Isaiah writes, "For since the beginning of the world men have not heard, nor perceived by the ear, neither hath the eye seen, O God, beside thee, what He hath prepared for him that waiteth for Him." (Isaiah 64:4)

With all of this inherent complexity, the next question is: why? God could have easily created a simple universe, without so many planets, stars, and galaxies. He could have created a handful of animals for food or to do work, but instead chose to create 1,500 species of starfish for instance. He could have also created a simplistic plant kingdom with only a few fruits and vegetables, but instead we have star fruit, pineapples, and peppers in a variety of colors. The option even exists to create hybrid species, such as a grapefruit or new varieties of apples.

Even more staggering is the reality that all of these things are constructed from a basic set of building blocks—atoms—and those atoms can be combined in a dizzying number of ways to create molecules. Molecules can then be used to build cells, bacteria, viruses, and more. Then there is the world of "programmable code" found in RNA and DNA.

Again, God did not *have* to create this level of complexity. Yes, there was a functional beauty involved but there was also joy in the act of creation. Consider some of these verses for example. In Revelation 4:11 it reads, "Thou art worthy, O Lord, to receive glory and honour and power: for thou hast created all things, and for thy pleasure they are and were created." In Psalm 104:24 – 26 it adds, "O Lord, how manifold are thy works! In wisdom hast thou made them all: the earth is full of thy riches. So is this great and wide sea, wherein are things creeping innumerable, both small and great beasts. There go the ships: there is that leviathan, whom thou hast made to play therein." In Job 38:7, God tells a bewildered Job that when the foundation of the earth was laid "the morning stars sang together, and all the sons of God shouted for joy."

Note the usage of the word "pleasure" in the first verse, "play" in the second, and "joy" in the third. If God takes joy in creation, why can't an artist join in the jubilation and create as an act of worship and faith? Throughout the rest of this book we will explore Biblical examples of how God has interacted with people through artistic and creative means. Perhaps, then, too, the word "creative" will become a part of the descriptive vocabulary of God.

- 2 -

The Artisans of the Tabernacle

"In the hearts of all that are wise hearted I have put wisdom, that they may make all that I have commanded thee." – Exodus 31:6

Sometimes we all need a tangible form of God's presence in our lives to reinforce our faith. Perhaps that is why, when the Israelites came up out of Egypt, God commanded Moses to build a portable tabernacle as a place for worship, sacrifice, and atonement. In Exodus 25:8 God said, "And let them make Me a sanctuary; that I may dwell among them." This was no simple sanctuary and not like previous altars that were often made of stone.

The pattern for the tabernacle was given to Moses by God on Mount Sinai, along with the Ten Commandments. This was not the first time God gave a plan directly to man, for He gave specific instructions to Noah on how to build an ark made of gopher wood. That plan seemed strictly practical in nature. This was also no ordinary exchange of ideas on God's part. Mount Sinai became enveloped in a cloud and God's glory appeared like a consuming fire on the mountaintop (Exodus 24:15 – 18). Moses then ascended the mountain and disappeared into the cloud for forty days and forty nights.

During that time, God described in great detail the plan for the tabernacle and how to build it. First, He told Moses to take offerings from the people in the form of metals (gold, silver, and bronze), linen, goat's hair, animal skins, wood, oil, spices, and stones. He then described how the materials were to be used, assembled, and placed. Finally, He informed Moses that He would be calling certain gifted artisans to carry out the work. As it turned out, the sanctuary took considerable skill to build and the diversity of the artisans involved was amazing.

The tabernacle consisted of a large rectangular area ringed by curtains, called the outer court, and an inner rectangular section which was further divided into the Holy Place and the Most Holy Place. Inside the Most Holy Place the Ark of the Covenant was stored, which included the stone tablets containing the Ten Commandments.

The Ark of the Covenant is described in Exodus 25:10 – 22. In Exodus 25:10 – 11 it states, "And they shall make an ark of shittim (acacia) wood: two cubits and a half shall be the length thereof, and a cubit and a half the breadth thereof, and a cubit and a half the height thereof. And thou shalt overlay it with pure gold, within and without shalt thou overlay it, and shalt make upon it a crown of gold round about." Then, in verse 18 it says, "And thou shalt make two cherubims of gold, of beaten work shalt thou make them, in the two ends of the mercy seat." The two cherubim faced each other with their wings outstretched.

What differentiated this object from an ordinary box was the use of gold and the incorporation of cherubim into the design. God could have told Moses to use plain wood and not bother with anything else. The implication is that this was to be a beautiful symbolic object as well as functional.

Likewise, the curtains for the tabernacle included cherubim in their design. They were composed of woven linen that used blue, purple, and scarlet thread. Linen originates from the flax plant, is difficult to weave, and is more expensive to produce compared to other materials. To process the flax, it is first harvested, soaked (retted), spread out, dried, beaten, and then spun into yarn. Again, God could have told Moses to use cheaper materials and not bother dyeing the fabric. Even the veil that separated the Holy Place from the Most Holy Place contained blue, purple, and scarlet thread as well as cherubim (Exodus 26:31). The door of the tabernacle also utilized the same thread colors.

The usage of vivid colors did not stop there. Aaron's priestly garments also used blue, purple, and scarlet thread along with gold. Gold was made into thread by hammering it into sheets and then cutting it apart. On the shoulders of the ephod were two onyx stones.

Six tribal names were engraved on one stone and six were engraved on the other. Both were then set in gold. "And thou shalt put the two stones upon the shoulders of the ephod for stones of memorial unto the children of Israel: and Aaron shall bear their names before the Lord upon his two shoulders for a memorial." (Exodus 28:12)

For Aaron's robe, God instructed Moses to make it all blue, with blue, purple, and scarlet pomegranates around its bottom hem. Yet God also said to alternate each pomegranate with a gold bell that would sound whenever he walked through the tabernacle. The reason for the bells is intriguing. In Exodus 28:35 it reads, "And it shall be upon Aaron to minister: and his sound shall be heard when he goeth in unto the holy place before the Lord, and when he cometh out, that he die not."

His breastplate was also a woven garment, designed with the same colors and again using gold. Gold chains also held up parts of his outfit, much like the gold rings and clasps that held up the curtains of the tabernacle. The breastplate also contained four rows of stones inscribed with the names of the tribes of Israel. The stones included sardius (carnelian), topaz, carbuncle, turquoise, sapphire, diamond, jacinth, agate, amethyst, beryl, onyx, and jasper. They were set into gold and located over Aaron's heart. Also over his heart the mysterious Urim and Thummim were attached, although it is unclear what they looked like. Perhaps the Urim and Thummim were stones or gems, but either way they were used in decision making (see Exodus 28:30, Numbers 27:21, 1 Samuel 28:6, and Ezra 2:63).

In Exodus 28:40, God gave instructions for garments for Aaron's sons. "And for Aaron's sons thou shalt make coats, and thou shalt make for them girdles, and bonnets shalt thou make for them, for glory and for beauty." The key words are at the end of the sentence—*for glory and for beauty.*

The artistic design of the tabernacle continued on into other realms as well. The golden lamp stand contained ornamental features that did not serve a functional purpose. It had seven lamps in all, but each lamp was molded like an almond blossom with an ornamental knob (Exodus 25:31 – 40). In Exodus 31 an altar of incense was described, again made of shittim (acacia) wood overlaid with gold. This altar stood inside the Holy Place and in front of the veil that divided the room from the Most Holy Place. It was rectangular in shape with a gold "crown" border on top and a horn on each of its corners. Would it have been easier to make a simple stand? Of course, but then it would not have been as unique or majestic.

The incense had a specific recipe, found in Exodus 30:34 – 35, that contained stacte, onycha, and galbanum mixed with frankincense. In verse 35 it states, "And thou shalt make it a perfume, a confection after the art of the apothecary, tempered together, pure and holy." Some translations include the word "salted" here as part of the creation process. The meanings of the words "stacte" and "onycha" are unclear, generally both being translated as types of resin that came from plants or sea life. Galbanum is a gum resin from yellow-flowered plants that grow in the Mediterranean region and frankincense is yet another resin that comes from a tree. God also instructed Moses to warn others not to attempt to imitate the incense recipe or use it for other purposes lest they be cut off from the people (Exodus 30:38).

The incense also served another unique and mysterious purpose—to shield Aaron on the Day of Atonement. In Leviticus 16:12 – 13, he was instructed to "Take a censer full of burning coals of fire from off the altar before the Lord, and his hands full of sweet incense beaten small, and bring it within the vail: and he shall put the incense upon the fire before the Lord, that the cloud of the incense may cover the mercy seat that is upon the testimony, that he die not." Sadly, in Leviticus 10:1 – 2, Aaron's own sons died because they offered "strange fire" which involved incense. It is possible this refers back to Exodus 30:9, where God warned about the altar of incense, "Ye shall offer no strange incense thereon, nor burnt sacrifice, nor meat offering; neither shall ye pour drink offering thereon."

Furthermore, God also gave a recipe for anointing oil in Exodus 30:23 – 25 which contained myrrh, cinnamon, calamus ("sweet-smelling cane" in NKJV), cassia, and olive oil. Like the incense, the anointing oil was created by the "art of the apothecary" (or a "perfumer" in other translations). Again, God warned if anyone made imitations of it or used it to anoint outsiders they would be cut off from the people (Exodus 30:33). It was used to anoint the tabernacle of meeting, the Ark of the Covenant, the showbread table and its utensils, the lamp stand and its utensils, the altar of incense, the laver, and the altar of burnt offering. It was also used on Aaron and his sons.

What is most striking about the tabernacle was that despite its heavy symbolism, it appealed to multiple senses at once. From the sights of the blue, purple, scarlet, and gold colors to the sounds of the bells on Aaron's robe to odors of the incense and anointing oil, it was meant to be an immersive sensory experience for anyone who set foot inside. It was a combination of metals, wood, fabric, stones, and animal skins that took artisans of considerable skill and experience to construct.

As mentioned earlier, God provided not only the plan but the workers to complete the job. In Exodus 31:2 – 5, God told Moses":

"See, I have called by name Bezaleel the son of Uri, the son of Hur, of the tribe of Judah: And I have filled him with the spirit of God, in wisdom, and in understanding, and in knowledge, and in all manner of workmanship, to devise cunning works, to work in gold, and in silver, and in brass, and in cutting of stones, to set them, and in carving of timber, to work in all manner of workmanship."

God also provided Aholiab, who was "an engraver, and a cunning workman, and an embroiderer in blue, and in purple, and in scarlet, and fine linen." (Exodus 38:23) God then provided other gifted artisans (Exodus 35:10) and stirred up the hearts of the people for the material offerings to build the tabernacle. In Exodus 35:21 it reads, "And they came, every one whose heart stirred him up, and every one whom his spirit made willing, and they brought the Lord's offering to the work of the tabernacle of the congregation, and for all his service, and for the holy garments." At the same time God gave Bezaleel and Aholiab teaching abilities and filled them both "with wisdom of heart, to work all manner of work, of the engraver, and of the cunning workman, and of the embroiderer, in blue, and in purple, in scarlet, and in fine linen, and of the weaver, even of them that do any work, and of those that devise cunning work." (Exodus 35:35)

Although God was the architect of the tabernacle that was ultimately built by human hands, we are told in Hebrews 8:5, Hebrews 8:10, and Hebrews 9:23 – 34 that the tabernacle, along with the Law and the Levitical priesthood, were merely shadows of heavenly things to come. Was this also the case with the arrangement of the tribes of Israel around the sanctuary?

In Numbers 2:1 – 34 it describes their configuration. The Levites were in the center, surrounding the tabernacle. The tribes of Dan, Asher, and Naphtali camped to the north, while Judah, Issachar, and Zebulun camped to the east. The tribes of Reuben, Simeon, and Gad camped to the south, while Ephraim, Manasseh, and Benjamin camped to the west. Although there is some debate as to the exact configuration of the surrounding tribes, one possibility is that the tribes were in the shape of a cross with the tabernacle being in the middle.

It is also interesting to note that once the earthly tabernacle was completed, the glory of the Lord filled it as a cloud. In Exodus 40:35 it reads, "And Moses was not able to enter into the tent of the congregation, because the cloud abode thereon, and the glory of the Lord filled the tabernacle." When the cloud lifted, the Israelites took down the tabernacle and journeyed on toward the Promised Land in Canaan. When the cloud descended, they stopped. At night, fire settled above the tabernacle so that it was "in the sight of all the house of Israel, throughout all their journeys." (Exodus 40:38)

Again, God did not need to go to such great lengths to manifest His presence. After all, this tabernacle was constructed after Moses led the Israelites out of Egypt via the Red Sea. The point is that He *chose* to dwell with them and *chose* to provide a continuous reminder of His glory in a way that involved all of one's senses.

- 3 -

The Temple Builders

"He has made everything beautiful in its time. Also He has put eternity in their hearts, except that no one can find out the work that God does from beginning to end." – Ecclesiastes 3:11

It started as a conversation between King David and the prophet Nathan while they were in David's house. David said, "See now, I dwell in an house of cedar, but the ark of God dwelleth within curtains." (2 Samuel 7:2) David was referring to the mobile tabernacle that Israel used at the time since Moses' days. Although it had made the journey into the Promised Land, the Israelites had since settled into the land.

That night, God spoke to the prophet Nathan and said, "Go and tell my servant David, Thus saith the Lord, 'Shalt thou build Me an house for Me to dwell in?'" (2 Samuel 7:5) God then told Nathan (to tell David) He had resided in a tent and a tabernacle ever since the Israelites came up out of Egypt. He then pointed out that He never once asked the Israelites to build Him a house of cedar (2 Samuel 7:7). The command then came forth that Solomon, David's son, would be the one to "build an house for My name, and I will stablish the throne of his kingdom for ever." (2 Samuel 7:13)

Excited, but remaining obedient to God, David gathered the officials from Israel and his son Solomon (1 Chronicles 28). He gave them instructions for building a magnificent temple. Like Moses and the tabernacle, God gave a pattern to David, but this time it was received in "his spirit" (verses 11 – 12). He then wrote down the plans and handed them over to Solomon (verse 19). David then provided iron, brass, masons, cedar (from Tyre and the Sidonians), and workers (1 Chronicles 22:2 – 4, 15). In 1 Chronicles 29:2 it reads, "Now I have prepared with all my might for the house of my God the gold for things to be made of gold, and the silver for things of silver, and the brass for things of brass, the iron for things of iron, and wood for things of wood; onyx stones, and stones to be set, glistering stones, and of divers colours, and all manner of precious stones, and marble stones in abundance."

The leaders of Israel also contributed willingly, "And gave for the service of the house of God of gold five thousand talents and ten thousand drams, and of silver ten thousand talents, and of brass eighteen thousand talents, and one hundred thousand talents of iron. And they with whom precious stones were found gave them to the treasure of the house of the Lord, by the hand of Jehiel the Gershonite." (1 Chronicles 29:7 – 8). The people then rejoiced along with David. David then encouraged Solomon to be strong and to be of good courage. He also provided Levites for service in the temple and craftsmen (1 Chronicles 28:20 – 21).

Why did God choose Solomon and not David to build the temple? Although God had given David peace with the surrounding nations, He told David, "Thou hast shed blood abundantly, and hast made great wars: thou shalt not build an house unto My name, because thou hast shed much blood upon the earth in My sight." (1 Chronicles 22:8)

Once David passed away and Solomon became king, Solomon started working on the temple. The temple was larger than the tabernacle and primarily built of stone and not wood and cloth. Although many portions of the temple and the artifacts within it were overlaid with gold, the wood was cedar (or cypress), in contrast to the acacia wood used in the tabernacle.

Solomon also reached out to Hiram I, the king of Tyre, and said, "Now therefore command thou that they hew me cedar trees out of Lebanon; and my servants shall be with thy servants: and unto thee will I give hire for thy servants according to all that thou shalt appoint: for thou knowest that there is not among us any that can skill to hew timber like unto the Sidonians." (1 Kings 5:6) Hiram responded favorably in exchange for wheat and pressed oil. He also sent over timber, workers, and "the son of a woman of the daughters of Dan" whose "father was a man of Tyre, skilful to work in gold, and in silver, in brass, in iron, in stone, and in timber, in purple, in blue, and in fine linen, and in crimson; also to grave any manner of graving." (2 Chronicles 2:13 – 14)

Solomon then created a massive labor force comprised of Israelites and foreigners. The size of the force was staggering. It included 30,000 from Israel (who were then sent to Lebanon in shifts), 70,000 carriers, 80,000 stonecutters, and 3,300 foremen/supervisors (1 Kings 5:13 – 16). In 1 Kings 5:18 it states that besides Solomon's builders, Hiram's builders and the Gebalites were involved. Yet in 1 Kings 9:15 – 22 it seems to indicate that although Solomon did not force the Israelites into labor, he did so with the Amorites, Hittites, Perizzites, Hivites, and Jebusites.

Some features of the temple were altered and exaggerated compared to the tabernacle. The main temple area grew to be 30 x 90 feet, and the Most Holy Place was increased in size to 30 x 30 x 30 feet (1 Kings 6:20). Two giant bronze pillars stood at the entrance to the temple and were twenty-seven feet high and eighteen feet in circumference. On the pillars were rows of pomegranates. Cherubim, palm trees, and flowers were then carved into the temple walls and doors and then overlaid with gold. Two giant olive-wood cherubim overlaid with gold were set on either side of the Ark of the Covenant in the Most Holy Place and their combined wingspans reached from one side of the room to the other. Instead of facing the Ark, as the cherubim on the Ark faced each other, they faced the entrance to the room and dwarfed the Ark (1 Kings 6:23 – 35).

The number of items in the temple was also multiplied. Instead of one lamp stand like the tabernacle, Solomon had ten lamp stands made. Instead of a single table for showbread, he created ten gold-plated bread tables. He even installed a set of gold-plated doors between the Holy Place and the Most Holy Place.

In 2 Chronicles 3:6, it states Solomon "garnished the house with precious stones for beauty" and in 2 Chronicles 3:14 that he created a veil of "blue, and purple, and crimson, and fine linen, and wrought cherubims thereon" at the entrance to the Most Holy Place in addition to the doors. Much like the tabernacle, some of the colors were retained as was the use of cherubim. Flowers (other than the lamp stand) were new additions along with the use of palm trees. There were also windows around the temple but their purpose was unknown. Oddly enough, no mention is made of creating any new priestly garments, similar to those that were made for Aaron and his sons. New to the temple was a giant "molten sea" (also known as the Brazen Sea), which consisted of a basin shaped like a lily blossom that rested on top of twelve oxen that faced outward. Its purpose was unknown.

Even though the temple took seven years to build, Solomon did not stop there. He created an entire complex of buildings that included his own house (which took thirteen years to build), the House of the Forest of Lebanon, and a house for Pharaoh's daughter, who was his wife. In the middle of the construction process, God spoke to Solomon and gave him a conditional promise. "Concerning this house which thou art in building, if thou wilt walk in My statutes, and execute My judgments, and keep all My commandments to walk in them; then will I perform My word with thee, which I spake unto David thy father: And I will dwell among the children of Israel, and will not forsake my people Israel." (1 Kings 6:12 – 13)

After the temple was finished, the Ark was brought in, and the glory of the Lord arrived afterward. In 1 Kings 8:10 – 11 it reads, "And it came to pass, when the priests were come out of the holy place, that the cloud filled the house of the Lord, so that the priests could not stand to minister because of the cloud: for the glory of the Lord had filled the house of the Lord." Solomon then blessed the Lord and dedicated the temple.

Despite the triumph of engineering and art, the splendor was short-lived. Solomon soon fell into idolatry and acquired multiple wives, horses, and massive amounts of silver and gold. Back in Deuteronomy 17:16 – 19, God specifically warned Israel's future kings against such things and for each king to read a copy of the Law all the days of his life so "that he may learn to fear the Lord his God, to keep all the words of this law and these statutes, to do them." (Deuteronomy 17:19) It is unclear whether Solomon did this, even though several portions of wisdom literature in the Scriptures are attributed to him.

Along with his own sinful nature, Solomon's multiple wives helped turn his heart away from the Lord. As a result, he built high places for the gods his wives worshipped. In 1 Kings 11:11 – 13 the

Lord told him, "Forasmuch as this is done of thee, and thou hast not kept My covenant and My statutes, which I have commanded thee, I will surely rend the kingdom from thee, and will give it to thy servant. Notwithstanding in thy days I will not do it for David thy father's sake: but I will rend it out of the hand of thy son."

After Solomon died, the rest of Israel split from Judah, and the people made Jeroboam their king (1 Kings 12). Jeroboam then created two golden calf idols and set them up in Bethel and Dan, so that the people no longer had to travel to Jerusalem to worship. Even worse, parts of the temple were looted or used to pay off debts. In 1 Kings 14:26, Shishak, king of Egypt, "took away the treasures of the house of the Lord, and the treasures of the king's house; he even took away all: and he took away all the shields of gold which Solomon had made." Later on, King Asa, who reigned in Judah from approximately 911 – 870 B.C., sent all the silver and gold that was left in the house of the Lord to Benhadad, the king of Syria, to pay off debts.

As kings came and went in both kingdoms, some turned the hearts of the people to idols while others tried to turn them back to the Lord. Eventually, the northern kingdom was attacked and many of its inhabitants were dragged away to Assyria (2 Kings 17). The southern kingdom fell, too, and they were carried away into exile by the Babylonians (2 Kings 25) which culminated in the destruction of Jerusalem in 586 – 587 B.C. The temple and all its furnishings were fully looted by Nebuchadnezzar and the Chaldean army (2 Kings 25:1 – 25).

While in exile in Babylon, Ezekiel, both a priest and a prophet, had numerous visions from the Lord, one of which described the glory of the Lord leaving the temple in Jerusalem (Ezekiel 8 – 10). He also had a vision for another temple (Ezekiel 40 – 48) which has never been built (more on this later).

Then, in the first year of the reign of King Cyrus II of Persia, God stirred the king's heart to allow the Israelites to return to their homeland and rebuild the temple at Jerusalem. Scripture does not indicate that a design plan was given by God this time, although Cyrus did send back many of the items that were originally looted from the temple by Nebuchadnezzar. The ones who returned were supported by others so that their hands were strengthened "with vessels of silver, with gold, with goods, and with beasts, and with precious things, beside all that was willingly offered." (Ezra 1:6)

No real description of the new temple is given in Scripture. No dimensions are listed and there is no mention of the artwork or the skills of the laborers involved. When the foundation was laid, the priests were given trumpets and the Levites were given cymbals. Together they sang and praised the Lord along with the people. Several of the priests and Levites who had seen the first temple wept while others shouted for joy. It is unclear why they wept but in Haggai 2:3 it indicates the new temple was much smaller than the previous one: "Who is left among you that saw this house in her first glory? And how do ye see it now? Is it not in your eyes in comparison of it as nothing?"

Also absent from the new temple is any mention of the Ark. Through the prophet Haggai, however, God reassures the people that someday His glory would return. "For thus saith the Lord of hosts; Yet once, it is a little while, and I will shake the heavens, and the earth, and the sea, and the dry land; And I will shake all nations, and the desire of all nations shall come: and I will fill this house with glory, saith the Lord of hosts." (Haggai 2:6 – 7) There is no mention of a glory cloud appearing in the new temple and many scholars have interpreted this as being fulfilled in the New Testament when Jesus entered the temple.

The construction of the new temple was also slow. It took sixteen years to build and the opposition to the rebuild was great. Numerous letters were sent back and forth between King Artaxerxes, Tattenai (a local governor), and King Darius of Persia before the harassment stopped (Ezra 4 – 7). Meanwhile, God encouraged the people to keep rebuilding by sending the prophets Haggai and Zechariah.

Then, around 19 or 20 B.C., Herod the Great ordered the demolition of the temple and rebuilt a larger one modeled after Solomon's original design (Hays, 140 – 141). He also expanded the temple mount and raised the height of the temple to 172 feet (100 cubits) in places. There were no windows and again there is no mention of a place for the Ark in Scripture. He included a Holy Place and a Most Holy Place, although the rooms were divided by a thick curtain and not doors. It is unknown from historical and Biblical sources what was actually stored in the Most Holy Place.

Although Herod led many construction projects around Jerusalem, it should be noted he was also responsible for the "Massacre of the Innocents". After Jesus was born, Herod was troubled and he consulted with the priests and the scribes. He also consulted with the wise men from the East. He told the wise men to "Go and search diligently for the young child; and when ye have found him, bring me word again, that I may come and worship him also." (Matthew 2:8)

After the wise men departed, they found Jesus but never returned to Herod because they were warned of Herod's intent in a dream. Angered, Herod issued an order to put to death all male children under the age of two years old in Bethlehem and the surrounding areas (Matthew 2:16 – 18). Joseph, Jesus' earthly father, had also been warned ahead of time in a dream to flee to Egypt with his family until the threat passed. Herod died a short time later and then Joseph brought his family back to Israel.

In 70 A.D., the Romans destroyed both the city of Jerusalem and the temple. This was prophesized by Jesus during a conversation with His disciples (Matthew 24:1 – 2; Mark 13:1 – 4; Luke 21:5 – 6). They commented on the marvelous architecture of the temple but He replied, "Seest thou these great buildings? There shall not be left one stone upon another, that shall not be thrown down." (Mark 13:2)

Since then, no temple has been rebuilt in Jerusalem although many efforts are underway to build one immediately should conditions allow for it. Many plans have been drawn up and utensils and other artifacts have been prepared. There have even been attempts to reinstitute the Sanhedrin, which, in former times, were assemblies of elders appointed as judges throughout the land of Israel.

This leaves us with a mystery. In the Book of Ezekiel, there are extensive and detailed plans of a third temple that has never been constructed (Ezekiel 40 – 48). In Ezekiel's vision from God, he was shown around the new temple by a man "whose appearance was like the appearance of brass, with a line of flax in his hand, and a measuring reed." (Ezekiel 40:3) The man then led Ezekiel throughout the temple, and measured its doorways, walls, and courts.

Like Solomon's temple, there were to be storage areas and galleries that spanned three floors (Ezekiel 41:16). The plans also mentioned narrow windows. There was also artwork which resembled Solomon's temple with some important changes and additions. In Ezekiel 41:18 – 19 we read, "And it was made with cherubims and palm trees, so that a palm tree was between a cherub and a cherub; and every cherub had two faces; so that the face of a man was toward the palm tree on the one side, and the face of a young lion toward the palm tree on the other side: it was made through all the house round about." This image is a unique evolution beyond the cherubim used in the tabernacle and Solomon's temple.

Again, there was to be a Holy Place and a Most Holy Place, and a command to build tables for offerings (Ezekiel 40:38 – 43) and chambers for the priests (Ezekiel 40:44 – 47). There is much debate amongst scholars about the purpose of the sacrifices and offerings mentioned in the vision since Jesus' sacrifice for sin did away for the need for them (Hebrews 9:11 – 28). Because of this, some hold a view that the temple is merely symbolic while others believe it will be built at the beginning of the Millennial Kingdom, when Christ is to reign on earth for 1,000 years (Revelation 20:1 – 6).

Others have commented that there is no Scriptural command to build the temple and that it was merely a representation of things in heaven or Jesus' sacrifice. There is a problem with that viewpoint because in Ezekiel 43:11 God told Ezekiel, "And if they [the Israelites] be ashamed of all that they have done, shew them the form of the house, and the fashion thereof, and the goings out thereof, and the comings in thereof, and all the forms thereof, and all the ordinances thereof, and all the forms thereof, and all the laws thereof: and write it in their sight, that they may keep the whole form thereof, and all the ordinances thereof, and do them." In other words, there seems to be a conditional command to build the temple that is dependent upon the repentance of the people.

Curiously, the prior chapters of the book describe a future Gog-Magog war that is unleashed against Israel (Ezekiel 38 – 39). Shame is mentioned in Ezekiel 39:26 and God says He will pour out His spirit on them so that "Neither will I hide My face any more from them: for I have poured out My spirit upon the house of Israel." (Ezekiel 39:29) Could this shame and repentance be the key that unlocks the building of Ezekiel's temple?

To add to the mystery, water flowed out from under the threshold of the temple toward both the Great Sea (the Mediterranean Sea) and the Dead Sea. The water that flowed toward the Dead Sea was an ever-deepening river that brought life wherever it went (Ezekiel 47:1

– 12, Zechariah 14:8). Going further, in Ezekiel 47:10 it says, "And it shall come to pass, that the fishers shall stand upon it from Engedi even unto Eneglaim; they shall be a place to spread forth nets; their fish shall be according to their kinds, as the fish of the great sea, exceeding many." En Gedi is on the shores of the Dead Sea while the location of Eneglaim (En Eglaim) is unknown. It also states that the marshes will be left for salt (Ezekiel 47:11). Currently the Dead Sea is just that—dead—and no fish can live in it due to its salinity and mineral content. Along the river there were also trees whose fruit never failed and whose leaves were to be used for medicine.

Lastly, in Ezekiel 43:1 – 5, like the tabernacle and Solomon's temple, the glory of the Lord arrived. The vision of the arrival was so dramatic it caused Ezekiel to fall onto his face (verse three).

There is one more significant place of worship mentioned in Scripture. This futuristic place (essentially a city) will one day come out of the clouds from heaven and is frequently referred to as the "New Jerusalem". Its description is found in Revelation 21 – 22, which starts with an unusual statement in verse one. "And I saw a new heaven and a new earth: for the first heaven and the first earth were passed away; and there was no more sea." (Revelation 21:1) As the city descended from heaven, the apostle John heard a voice out of heaven saying, "Behold, the tabernacle of God is with men, and he will dwell with them, and they shall be his people, and God himself shall be with them, and be their God." (Revelation 21:3)

The wall around the city will have twelve gates. Each gate will have an angel and a name of a tribe of Israel written on it (Revelation 21:12). The wall will also have twelve foundations, one for each of the apostles (Revelation 21:14). Again, like in Ezekiel's vision, John saw a man with a measuring rod and "the building of the wall of it was of jasper: and the city was pure gold, like unto clear glass." (Revelation 21:18) The foundations of the wall will be decorated with twelve types of stones (echoing back to the stones embedded on Aaron's breastplate).

The gates will also be made of pearl and streets in the city will be pure gold. John used the term "transparent glass" to describe the gold. An interesting property of gold is that when it is ground into finer and finer particles it changes color. If it is suspended in a liquid, also known as colloidal gold, it can be colored red, blue, purple, or even black. At the nanoparticle size it can even be transparent.

Yet this city is also described as *not* having a temple. In Revelation 21:22 it reads, "And I saw no temple therein: for the Lord God Almighty and the Lamb are the temple of it." Then in verse 23 it states, "And the city had no need of the sun, neither of the moon, to shine in it: for the glory of God did lighten it, and the Lamb is the light thereof." A river with trees is also described. "And he shewed me a pure river of water of life, clear as crystal, proceeding out of the throne of God and of the Lamb. In the midst of the street of it, and on either side of the river, was there the tree of life, which bare twelve manner of fruits, and yielded her fruit every month: and the leaves of the tree were for the healing of the nations." (Revelation 22:1 – 2)

Individually, the tabernacle and the temples share places for a Holy Place and a Most Holy Place. What is curious is a comparison of the dimensions throughout each era. Although there is some debate, in the tabernacle the Most Holy Place was considered to be about 15 x 15 x 15 feet (a cube). In Solomon's temple, the size of the room was expanded to approximately 20 x 20 x 20 cubits (or 30 – 35 feet approximately). In other words, it was another cube.

The dimensions of the Most Holy Place in the second temple are unknown until Herod rebuilt the structure. Estimates for the room size are around 34 x 34 feet with the ceiling height again being subject to interpretation. If we then compare it to the temple found in Ezekiel's vision, the size of the Most Holy Place is listed as being 20 x 20 cubits (Ezekiel 41:4). Depending on which measurement for a cubit that is used, it would be approximately 35 x 35 feet (20 cubits x 21 inches per cubit) or around the same size as Solomon's temple. No height is given in the text.

Now, if we put these all these geometric representations next to the New Jerusalem an interesting pattern emerges. In Revelation 21:16 we are told "The city lieth foursquare, and the length is as large as the breadth: and he measured the city with the reed, twelve thousand furlongs. The length and the breadth and the height of it are equal." Twelve thousand furlongs (12,000 stadia in the NIV translation) is equivalent to approximately 7,281,000 feet, if we use a measure of 606 feet and 9 inches per furlong. Converting to miles makes it about 1,378 miles *per side* on this city. Since the length, breadth, and height are all equal, that makes it either a gigantic cube or a pyramid (due to the foundational walls it seems more likely that it is a cube). Is this just a continuation of the Most Holy Place as found in the tabernacle and the temples? Is that what the Most Holy Place was supposed to represent all along?

Finally, when discussing temple structures in Scripture, Jesus and Paul also referred to people as being temples. Jesus referred to His own body as a temple and also that He was greater than the physical temple building itself. In John 2:18 – 22, after He cleared the temple in Jerusalem of moneychangers, the Jews gathered there asked Him for a sign. He replied, "Destroy this temple, and in three days I will raise it up." (John 2:19) John then explained that while the Jews thought He was referring to the physical temple building, in reality He was referring to His own body and what they would do to it. Jesus even went further in Matthew 12:6, while debating with the Pharisees about the Sabbath, and stated, "But I say unto you, that in this place is one greater than the temple."

Before Jesus' crucifixion, when He was brought before Caiaphas and the council of scribes and elders, they sought to find false witnesses to testify. Although they struggled to find any, two eventually came forward and said, "This fellow said, 'I am able to destroy the temple of God, and to build it in three days." (Matthew 26:61) This accusation was then hurled at Jesus again even while He hung on the cross. In Matthew 27:40 several bystanders yelled, "Thou that destroyest the temple, and buildest it in three days, save thyself. If thou be the Son of God, come down from the cross."

Jesus, of course, went on to die only to be resurrected three days later. In the physical temple, however, when He died an intriguing event occurred. "And, behold, the veil of the temple was rent in twain from the top to the bottom; and the earth did quake, and the rocks rent." (Matthew 27:51) There were two curtains in Herod's temple and it is unclear which curtain was torn, although many believe it was the one between the Holy Place and the Most Holy Place.

Later, the apostle Paul also expanded on the body-as-a-temple concept. In 1 Corinthians 6:19 – 20 he wrote, "What? Know ye not that your body is the temple of the Holy Ghost which is in you, which ye have of God, and ye are not your own? For ye are bought with a price: therefore glorify God in your body, and in your spirit, which are God's." In 1 Corinthians 3:16 – 17 he warned, "Know ye not that ye are the temple of God, and that the Spirit of God dwelleth in you? If any man defile the temple of God, him shall God destroy; for the temple of God is holy, which temple ye are."

He then goes even further by stating that Christians as a whole form a temple with Jesus being the "chief cornerstone" (Ephesians 2:19 – 22). In Ephesians 2:22 he wrote that we are "builded together for an habitation of God through the Spirit."

Can comparisons then be drawn between the physical tabernacle, the temples, and the human body? Possibly. What is clear, though, is that the physical temples had features, much like the tabernacle, that involved artistic skill. Although the cherubim and palm trees likely had symbolic significance, their beauty was much greater than any functional value.

- 4 -

The Writers

"Thy word is a lamp unto my feet, and a light unto my path." – Psalm 119:105

    Now let us take a look at another form of art in the Bible—the written word. First, let's start with what the Bible says about itself. As mentioned earlier, in John 1:1 it reads, "In the beginning was the Word, and the Word was with God, and the Word was God" and in verse fourteen it states, "and the Word was made flesh, and dwelt among us, (and we beheld His glory, the glory as of the only begotten of the Father,) full of grace and truth." In short, Jesus was the Word made flesh and He has existed since the beginning of time.

    God's Word is also compared to a fire and a hammer in Jeremiah 23:29: "Is not my word like as a fire? Saith the Lord; and like a hammer that breaketh the rock in pieces?" In Hebrews 4:12 it states, "For the word of God is quick, and powerful, and sharper than any twoedged sword, piercing even to the dividing asunder of soul and spirit, and of the joints and marrow, and is a discerner of the thoughts and intents of the heart." In Psalm 119:105 it reads, "Thy word is a lamp unto my feet, and a light unto my path." If that was not enough, in Isaiah 55:11 the Lord says, "So shall My word be that goeth forth out of My mouth: it shall not return unto Me void, but it shall accomplish that which I please, and it shall prosper in the thing whereto I sent it."

    A fire, a hammer, a sword, a lamp, and alive. In essence, the Bible is composed of words that are directly empowered by God Himself and have impact regardless of the situation. The Word also illuminates the way. In Matthew 24:35 Jesus added, "Heaven and earth shall pass away, but My words shall not pass away." So, not only is the Word vital for our time, but it transcends time and is ultimately eternal.

How powerful it must have been then for Moses to witness God writing the Ten Commandments with His own finger on two tablets of stone: "And He gave unto Moses, when He had made an end of communing with him upon mount Sinai, two tables of testimony, tables of stone, written with the finger of God." (Exodus 31:18) It is interesting to note that the tablets had writing on both sides as it illustrates in Exodus 32:15: "And Moses turned, and went down from the mount, and the two tables of the testimony were in his hand: the tables were written on both their sides; on the one side and on the other were they written."

Unfortunately when Moses came down from Mount Sinai he found the Israelites, led by Aaron, dancing in front of an idolatrous golden calf. In a fit of anger, he broke the tablets (Exodus 32:19) but God later told him to "Hew thee two tables of stone like unto the first: and I will write upon these tables the words that were in the first tables, which thou brakest." (Exodus 34:1)

But what about all the other words that God told the various prophets and apostles to write down over the centuries? Where did they all come from? Granted every writer in the Bible had their own style, yet in 2 Peter 1:20 – 21 we are told, "Knowing this first, that no prophecy of the scripture is of any private interpretation. For the prophecy came not in old time by the will of man: but holy men of God spake as they were moved by the Holy Ghost". In 2 Timothy 3:16, Paul wrote, "All scripture is given by inspiration of God, and is profitable for doctrine, for reproof, for correction, for instruction in righteousness." In other words, God gave them the text and it was each writer's responsibility to write the information down.

Another major Old Testament prophet, Jeremiah, described what it was like to receive words from God and the difficulty that came with it. In Jeremiah 20:8 – 9 he wrote, "For since I spake, I cried out, I cried violence and spoil; because the word of the Lord was made a reproach unto me, and a derision, daily. Then I said, I will not make mention of Him, nor speak any more in His name. But His word was in mine heart as a burning fire shut up in my bones, and I was weary with forbearing, and I could not stay." Have you ever been given direction or information from God and then kept silent? How did that go? Jeremiah had many unpopular prophecies and declarations from God to say to his people and they were rarely well received.

Like Moses and the broken tablets, Jeremiah the prophet and his scribe, Baruch, went through a "rewrite process" with God. In Jeremiah 36, there is a confrontation between the Word of God and King Jehoiakim, who reigned in Judah from 609 – 598 B.C. It is an example of a "Bible burning" within the Bible itself. In verse two, God commanded Jeremiah to take a scroll and write down all He had told the prophet "from the days of Josiah, even unto this day." Jeremiah then contacted Baruch, the son of Neriah, who wrote down Jeremiah's words and then read the scroll in the temple at Jerusalem.

The words were then relayed to several princes and scribes who were gathered in the scribe's chamber of the king's house. They called for Baruch and asked him to reread the scroll in their presence. Baruch complied. Then they told him they would repeat everything to the king. They also told Baruch to go and hide, along with Jeremiah (verses 8 – 19).

They told the king who in turn told them to get the scroll and to read it in his presence (verses 20 – 21). Every time a few columns were read, the king cut out that portion of the scroll and threw it into his fireplace (verses 22 – 23). In the end, the entire scroll was consumed. The king then commanded that Baruch and Jeremiah be seized but "but the Lord hid them." (verse 26)

In verse 28, God told Jeremiah, "Take thee again another roll, and write in it all the former words that were in the first roll, which Jehoiakim the king of Judah hath burned." Jeremiah and Baruch complied and "there were added besides unto them many like words." (verse 32) As for the king, God declared, "He shall have none to sit upon the throne of David: and his dead body shall be cast out in the day to the heat, and in the night to the frost. And I will punish him and his seed and his servants for their iniquity; and I will bring upon them, and upon the inhabitants of Jerusalem, and upon the men of Judah, all the evil that I have pronounced against them; but they hearkened not." (verses 30 – 31)

What about the other prophets that God called to "write down His words"? A prophet had to be careful when quoting what God said. In fact, in the Old Testament the penalty for false prophecies was death. "But the prophet, which shall presume to speak a word in My name, which I have not commanded him to speak, or that shall speak in the name of other gods, even that prophet shall die." (Deuteronomy 18:20) Even in the New Testament, John soberly warned, "For I testify unto every man that heareth the words of the prophecy of this book, if any man shall add unto these things, God shall add unto him the plagues that are written in this book: and if any man shall take away from the words of the book of this prophecy, God shall take away his part out of the book of life, and out of the holy city, and from the things which are written in this book." (Revelation 22:18 – 19)

Strangely enough, though, there are a couple of instances where God told an apostle or a prophet *not* to write everything down. Daniel 12:4 reads, "But thou, O Daniel, shut up the words, and seal the book, even to the time of the end: many shall run to and fro, and knowledge shall be increased." In Revelation 10:3, in between the sounding of the sixth and the seventh trumpets, John wrote about hearing "seven thunders". "And when the seven thunders had uttered their voices, I was about to write: and I heard a voice from heaven saying unto me, 'Seal up those things which the seven thunders uttered, and write them not.'" (Revelation 10:4) Despite the extensive details elsewhere in prophecy, not everything was ready to be revealed.

There is even a pair of ironic verses in the Book of Job, whose authorship is unknown. In Job 19:23 – 24 Job lamented, "Oh that my words were now written! Oh that they were printed in a book! That they were graven with an iron pen and lead in the rock for ever!" These lines are then followed by one of the more famous verses from the book, "For I know that my redeemer liveth, and that He shall stand at the latter day upon the earth." (verse 25) Then, in Job 31:35 – 36 he stated, "Oh that one would hear me! Behold, my desire is, that the Almighty would answer me, and that mine adversary had written a book. Surely I would take it upon my shoulder, and bind it as a crown to me."

In the New Testament, Saul of Tarsus, who later became known as the apostle Paul, was another Biblical figure whose interactions with the Lord are instructive. In Acts 9, after Saul oversaw the stoning of Stephen (Acts 6:8 – 7:60), persecuted the early Christian church, and was "yet breathing out threatenings and slaughter against the disciples of the Lord" (Acts 9:1) he was confronted by Jesus on the road to Damascus. A light shone around him from heaven followed by a voice that said, "Saul, Saul, why persecutest thou me?" (Acts 9:4) After Saul responded, Jesus then said, "Arise, and go into the city, and it shall be told thee what thou must do." (Acts 9:6)

Those who accompanied Saul did not see anybody but they heard the voice. Saul arose and was led into the city where his sight was restored three days later through the laying on of hands by Ananias (Acts 9:9 – 18). His name was also eventually changed to Paul.

Although Paul is credited with writing the Book of Romans through the Book of Hebrews (there is some debate about who authored Hebrews, however), he referred to himself as "the least of the apostles, that am not meet to be called an apostle, because I persecuted the church of God." (1 Corinthians 15:9) He also played down his verbal abilities in 2 Corinthians 11:4 – 6, where he compared himself to other "preachers" in the area saying, "For if he that cometh preacheth another Jesus, whom we have not preached, or if ye receive another spirit, which ye have not received, or another gospel, which ye have not accepted, ye might well bear with him. For I suppose I was not a whit behind the very chiefest apostles. But though I be rude in speech, yet not in knowledge; but we have been throughly made manifest among you in all things." Again in 2 Corinthians 12:11 – 12 he added, "I am become a fool in glorying; ye have compelled me: for I ought to have been commended of you: for in nothing am I behind the very chiefest apostles, though I be nothing. Truly the signs of an apostle were wrought among you in all patience, in signs, and wonders, and mighty deeds."

What is ironic is that Paul's words survived while theirs did not. This is due to the fact that his words came from Jesus Christ. In Galatians 1:11 – 12 he wrote, "But I certify you, brethren, that the gospel which was preached of me is not after man. For I neither received it of man, neither was I taught it, but by the revelation of Jesus Christ." Even after this revelation he did not immediately return to Jerusalem. He instead went to Arabia and then went to Damascus. Only after three years passed did he go to Jerusalem to meet with Peter (Galatians 1:15 – 18).

God's interaction with writers does not end there. From Genesis to

Revelation, there is interplay between the Creator and human writers. For example, in Revelation 2:1 – 3:22, Jesus told the apostle John to write down seven letters to be given to seven churches in the region. In the Gospels we also see Jesus going back and forth with the scribes of His day, although the interaction was often unpleasant.

In Ancient Israel, few people received training in the art of writing. Of the ones that did, they were called scribes and were considered scholars who could even hold civic offices. Not only did they translate and copy Biblical manuscripts, but in the era of the Second Temple they became teachers and interpreters of the Law of Moses. In the Gospels, they were associated with both the Sadducees and the Pharisees and were considered scholars. They often challenged Jesus. For instance, in Mark 2:16 – 17 it reads, "And when the scribes and Pharisees saw Him eat with publicans and sinners, they said unto His disciples, 'How is it that He eateth and drinketh with publicans and sinners?'" Jesus then replied, "They that are whole have no need of the physician, but they that are sick: I came not to call the righteous, but sinners to repentance." (Mark 2:17)

In Matthew 23, right before Jesus predicted the destruction of the temple in Jerusalem, He spoke to the disciples and the multitude in the temple about the scribes and the Pharisees. In His discourse, He exposed their hypocrisy by comparing their inner character with their outward actions and appearance. First, He acknowledged that "the scribes and the Pharisees sit in Moses' seat." (Matthew 23:2) Then He called them out on their hypocrisy and said, "All therefore whatsoever they bid you observe, that observe and do; but do not ye after their works: for they say, and do not. For they bind heavy burdens and grievous to be borne, and lay them on men's shoulders; but they themselves will not move them with one of their fingers." (Matthew 23:3 – 4)

He then listed the ways they craved public recognition and attention (even to the point of enlarging the borders on their garments) yet how they "shut up the kingdom of heaven against men" (verse 13). He then declared several "woes" unto the scribes and Pharisees related to their actions versus their inner character. He ended the discourse with a severe condemnation, saying:

"Wherefore, behold, I send unto you prophets, and wise men, and scribes: and some of them ye shall kill and crucify; and some of them shall ye scourge in your synagogues, and persecute them from city to city: that upon you may come all the righteous blood shed upon the earth, from the blood of righteous Abel unto the blood of Zacharias son of Barachias, whom ye slew between the temple and the altar. Verily I say unto you, all these things shall come upon this generation." (Matthew 23:34 – 36)

An example of a scribe that was sent during the building of the Second Temple was Ezra the priest, who was "a ready scribe in the law of Moses" (Ezra 7:6) and "had prepared his heart to seek the law of the Lord, and to do it, and to teach in Israel statutes and judgments." (Ezra 7:10) Yet the scribes in Jesus' time were more interested in self-preservation despite travelling great distances in order to gain a convert (Matthew 23:15).

Many of these scribes and elders were also present at Jesus' final stand before Caiaphas the high priest and the Sanhedrin. False testimony against Jesus was sought and He was accused of blasphemy by Caiaphas (Matthew 26:57 – 65). After saying Jesus was deserving of death (Matthew 26:66), "Then did they spit in His face, and buffeted Him; and others smote Him with the palms of their hands, saying, 'Prophesy unto us, thou Christ, Who is he that smote thee?'" (Matthew 26:67 – 68) It is unclear who spit at Him and who hit Him, but some of the scribes were likely involved.

Despite their attacks their persecution was temporary. Jesus died and rose again and will always have the final word. For "The grass withereth, the flower fadeth: but the word of our God shall stand for ever." (Isaiah 40:8) Finally, in Revelation 22:13 Jesus emphatically stated, "I am Alpha and Omega, the beginning and the end, the first and the last." It's not every day that you find an author who lives eternally and whose book will never go out of print.

- 5 -

The Actors, Sculptors, and Dancers

"Praise Him with the timbrel and dance: praise Him with stringed instruments and organs." – Psalm 150:4

In addition to being called by God to write down words, some prophets were instructed to take things a step further and portray dramatic events. Two major prophets, Jeremiah and Ezekiel, were called to act out God's proclamations in strange and unusual ways.

For example, Jeremiah was called to put on a linen sash and then travel to the Euphrates River (Jeremiah 13:1 – 4). God then told him to stuff the sash in a hole in a rock. A few days later God directed him to retrieve the sash. Jeremiah found it ruined and God then told him:

> "After this manner will I mar the pride of Judah, and the great pride of Jerusalem. This evil people, which refuse to hear My words, which walk in the imagination of their heart, and walk after other gods, to serve them, and to worship them, shall even be as this girdle, which is good for nothing. For as the girdle cleaveth to the loins of a man, so have I caused to cleave unto Me the whole house of Israel and the whole house of Judah, saith the Lord; that they might be unto Me for a people, and for a name, and for a praise, and for a glory: but they would not hear." (Jeremiah 13:9 – 11)

This, of course, was a visual pronouncement of judgment on Israel and Judah after years of turning their backs on God.

In Jeremiah 19:1 – 15, God directed Jeremiah to take a potter's

Gathering the Artists

earthen flask (or bottle) and bring some elders and priests with him to the Valley of the Son of Hinnom. Much like the linen sash demonstration, God told Jeremiah to pronounce catastrophe on Judah and Jerusalem for their years of rampant idolatry and child sacrifice to Baal (verses 3 – 9). Jeremiah then broke the flask and said, "Thus saith the Lord of hosts; 'Even so will I break this people and this city, as one breaketh a potter's vessel, that cannot be made whole again: and they shall bury them in Tophet, till there be no place to bury. Thus will I do unto this place, saith the Lord, and to the inhabitants thereof, and even make this city as Tophet.'" (Jeremiah 19:11 – 12) Needless to say, much of Jeremiah's pronouncements, including this drama, were quite unpopular.

In Jeremiah 27, God then commanded the prophet to put "bonds and yokes on his neck" and to "send them to the king of Edom, and to the king of Moab, and to the king of the Ammonites, and to the king of Tyrus, and to the king of Zidon, by the hand of the messengers which come to Jerusalem unto Zedekiah king of Judah." (verse three) Jeremiah then told them these nations must come under the yoke of King Nebuchadnezzar of Babylon or the Lord would turn them over to death by sword, famine, and pestilence.

Jeremiah also warned them about false prophets that lied to the people by declaring that God would not bring judgment upon Judah. One such false prophet was named Hananiah, who claimed that God would "break the yoke of the king of Babylon" (Jeremiah 28:4) and would bring back the exiles in two years. Jeremiah was initially agreeable and Hananiah took the yoke off Jeremiah's neck and broke it.

God was not pleased, however, and told Jeremiah to tell Hananiah, "Thus saith the Lord, 'Thou hast broken the yokes of wood; but thou shalt make for them yokes of iron.'" (Jeremiah 28:13) Jeremiah then told him, "The Lord hath not sent thee; but thou makest this people to trust in a lie. Therefore thus saith the Lord, 'Behold, I will cast thee from off the face of the earth: this year thou shalt die, because thou hast taught rebellion against the Lord.'" (Jeremiah 28:15 – 16) As a result, Hananiah died later that year and the exiles did not come back within two years.

In a likewise manner, God also had Ezekiel act out numerous dramas in the presence of others in order to make a point. In Ezekiel

4:1, God instructed the prophet to:

> "Take thee a tile, and lay it before thee, and pourtray upon it the city, even Jerusalem: and lay siege against it, and build a fort against it, and cast a mount against it; set the camp also against it, and set battering rams against it round about. Moreover take thou unto thee an iron pan, and set it for a wall of iron between thee and the city: and set thy face against it, and it shall be besieged, and thou shalt lay siege against it. This shall be a sign to the house of Israel." (Ezekiel 4:1 – 3) Then God had Ezekiel lay on his left side for 390 days in order to bear the iniquity of the house of Israel, with each day representing a year. He then told Ezekiel to lay on his right side for forty days, again with each day representing a year, for the iniquity of Judah (Ezekiel 4:4 – 6).

Ezekiel was then told to prepare a special recipe of bread made from wheat, barley, beans, lentils, millet, and spelt (Ezekiel 4:9) and to prepare a measure of water daily. He was told to bake his bread using human waste for fuel (Ezekiel 4:12) to which the prophet objected. God then told him to use cow dung instead. God then explained the intended outcome by saying, "Son of man, behold, I will break the staff of bread in Jerusalem: and they shall eat bread by weight, and with care; and they shall drink water by measure, and with astonishment: That they may want bread and water, and be astonied one with another, and consume away for their iniquity." (Ezekiel 4:16 – 17) Talk about taking unpleasant directions from the Director!

If that was not dramatic enough, God then told Ezekiel:

> "Take thee a sharp knife, take thee a barber's razor, and cause it to pass upon thine head and upon thy beard: then take thee balances to weigh, and divide the hair. Thou shalt burn with fire a third part in the midst of the city, when the days of the siege are fulfilled: and thou shalt take a third part, and smite about it with a knife: and a third part thou shalt scatter in the wind; and I will draw out a sword after them. Thou shalt also take thereof a few in number, and bind them in thy skirts. Then take of them again, and cast them into the midst of the fire, and burn them in the fire; for thereof

shall a fire come forth into all the house of Israel." (Ezekiel 5:1 – 4)

Again, like Jeremiah's prophecies, these actions were visual demonstrations of God's judgments on Jerusalem. In Ezekiel 5:12 He made it clearer by saying, "A third part of thee shall die with the pestilence, and with famine shall they be consumed in the midst of thee: and a third part shall fall by the sword round about thee; and I will scatter a third part into all the winds, and I will draw out a sword after them."

Judah's future captivity was also portrayed when the prophet packed up his belongings in preparation for exile (Ezekiel 12:1 – 6). He was then told to dig through a wall at twilight and carry his belongings on his shoulders as a sign to Israel. God then told Ezekiel that "The prince that is among them shall bear upon his shoulder in the twilight, and shall go forth: they shall dig through the wall to carry out thereby: he shall cover his face, that he see not the ground with his eyes. My net also will I spread upon him, and he shall be taken in my snare: and I will bring him to Babylon to the land of the Chaldeans; yet shall he not see it, though he shall die there." (Ezekiel 12:12 – 13)

Despite all these enactments, God had yet another symbol for the house of Israel. This time, unfortunately, it involved Ezekiel's wife. The Lord told Ezekiel that his wife was going to die but told him not to mourn or weep for her (Ezekiel 24:15 – 16). In Ezekiel 24:17, God commanded him to "Forbear to cry, make no mourning for the dead, bind the tire of thine head upon thee, and put on thy shoes upon thy feet, and cover not thy lips, and eat not the bread of men." The logic of such withholding of grief is then explained in verses 21 – 24.

In these examples, God used drama to make His point. With Jeremiah and Ezekiel, the demonstrations symbolized judgment but the message had greater impact than just words alone.

Like the broken potter's flask, God also used pottery as a symbol in several places in the Bible. In Jeremiah 18, he sent the prophet to a potter's house to observe the creation of an object on the potter's wheel. "'Arise, and go down to the potter's house, and there I will cause thee to hear My words.' Then I went down to the potter's house, and, behold, he wrought a work on the wheels. And the vessel that he made of clay was marred in the hand of the potter: so he made it again another vessel, as seemed good to the potter to make it." (Jeremiah 18:2 – 4)

Essentially, a potter's wheel consisted of a disc-shaped spinning platform upon which a potter would drop a piece of clay and then use their hands (or small carving tools) to shape and mold the clay into a pot, bowl, or other artifact. It took time, patience, water, hands, and clay to create a useful or artistic object which would then be fired in a kiln to harden its shape. What starts out as a drab brown or gray lump of clay can be thrown into a magnificent piece of art in minutes with skilled hands.

In Jeremiah 18:6, God told Jeremiah, "O house of Israel, cannot I do with you as this potter? Saith the Lord. Behold, as the clay is in the potter's hand, so are ye in Mine hand, O house of Israel." God then explained if Israel repented He would relent from the disaster that was about to overtake them. Isaiah 64:8 reinforced the pot-and-potter symbolism by stating, "But now, O Lord, thou art our Father; we are the clay, and thou our potter; and we all are the work of Thy hand." Israel, of course, did not repent.

This type of symbolism was carried on into the New Testament in Paul's writings. In Romans 9:20 – 21, in the middle of a discourse about Israel's rejection of Christ and its consequences, he said, "Nay but, O man, who art thou that repliest against God? Shall the thing formed say to Him that formed it, Why hast thou made me thus? Hath not the potter power over the clay, of the same lump to make one vessel unto honour, and another unto dishonour?" Paul then explained that Israel had not attained the Law of righteousness because "they sought it not by faith" (Romans 9:32).

In 2 Corinthians 4:7 – 10, he portrayed individuals as being "earthen vessels", adding, "But we have this treasure in earthen vessels, that the excellency of the power may be of God, and not of us. We are troubled on every side, yet not distressed; we are perplexed, but not in despair; persecuted, but not forsaken; cast down, but not destroyed; always bearing about in the body the dying of the Lord Jesus, that the life also of Jesus might be made manifest in our body." Here, Paul juxtaposed the spiritual hope one has in Christ in contrast with the physical body. Being "troubled on every side, yet not distressed" and "perplexed but not in despair" speaks to the hope one has inside despite external opposition and tribulation.

To the worldly observer, this makes no sense and is intriguing at the same time. Circumstances that would crush a normal person become opportunities for growth in the hands of God. Like a clay pot on the wheel, external events shape the life of a Christian but it is the Holy Spirit's strength inside that gives endurance. "For which cause we faint not; but though our outward man perish, yet the inward man is renewed day by day. For our light affliction, which is but for a moment, worketh for us a far more exceeding and eternal weight of glory." (2 Corinthians 4:16 – 17)

Not to be left out, dance appears in a few places in the Bible – most notably in the Psalms and in the life of King David. In Psalm 149:1 – 3 it reads, "Praise ye the Lord. Sing unto the Lord a new song, and His praise in the congregation of saints. Let Israel rejoice in Him that made Him: let the children of Zion be joyful in their King. Let them praise His name in the dance: let them sing praises unto Him with the timbrel and harp." Psalm 150:4 echoes a similar theme by stating, "Praise Him with the timbrel and dance: praise Him with stringed instruments and organs." More famously, Ecclesiastes 3:4 tells us there is a "time to weep, and a time to laugh; a time to mourn, and a time to dance."

Dance is also mentioned in the context of celebration. In Jeremiah 31:13 it reads, "Then shall the virgin rejoice in the dance, both young men and old together: for I will turn their mourning into joy, and will comfort them, and make them rejoice from their sorrow." This referred to the return of the Israelites from captivity in Babylon, but may also be a prophecy of a future event. Is it any type of dance? No. These verses refer to dancing as a means of praise, jubilation, and glorifying God.

This type of artistic expression was also demonstrated back in 2 Samuel 6, when the Ark of the Covenant was brought into Jerusalem after a long absence. Once an object of great power and reverence, it seemed the Ark spent some time in the house of Abinadab rather than being housed in the temple (2 Samuel 6:1 – 4).

David and others played music on multiple instruments in celebration as the Ark made its way to the city. "And David danced before the Lord with all his might; and David was girded with a linen ephod. So David and all the house of Israel brought up the ark of the Lord with shouting, and with the sound of the trumpet." (2 Samuel

6:14 – 15) Not everyone enjoyed the moment. Michal, Saul's daughter and David's wife, "looked through a window, and saw King David leaping and dancing before the Lord; and she despised him in her heart." (2 Samuel 6:16)

Michal eventually confronted him and said, "How glorious was the king of Israel to day, who uncovered himself to day in the eyes of the handmaids of his servants, as one of the vain fellows shamelessly uncovereth himself!" (2 Samuel 6:20) David rebuked her and replied, "It was before the Lord, which chose me before thy father, and before all his house, to appoint me ruler over the people of the Lord, over Israel: therefore will I play before the Lord. And I will yet be more vile than thus, and will be base in mine own sight: and of the maidservants which thou hast spoken of, of them shall I be had in honour." (2 Samuel 6:21 – 22) Michal was then said to have "no child unto the day of her death." (2 Samuel 6:23)

Although the Word is by far the most prevalent means God has used to communicate, He has shown there are no limits to His creativity even if it meant pushing the prophets to dramatic extremes. Often, too, drama and dance do not exist alone and are accompanied by music. In the next chapter we'll explore the two-way creative method of praise and communication called music.

- 6 -

The Musicians

"And He hath put a new song in my mouth, even praise unto our God: many shall see it, and fear, and shall trust in the Lord." – Psalm 40:3

    The earliest appearance of music in Scripture is found in the Book of Genesis. In Genesis 4:19 – 21, we learn of a couple, Lamech and Adah, who had two sons together. Note, this is not the same as Noah's father, Lamech, but Lamech was a distant descendent of Cain. The first son borne to Lamech was Jabal, who was the "the father of such as dwell in tents, and of such as have cattle." (Genesis 4:20) The other son was Jubal, who was the "father of all such as handle the harp and organ." (Genesis 4:21) In the NIV translation, the words "harp and organ" are rendered "stringed instruments and pipes". Jubal was also the half-brother of Tubal-Cain, through Lamech's other wife, Zillah. Tubal-Cain was an "instructer of every artificer in brass and iron" (Genesis 4:22). In other translations, he is listed as being a "forger of instruments" or tools in bronze and iron.

    From this point until the introduction of David, there are only sporadic examples of music mentioned in Scripture. I will address some of those instances throughout the rest of this book. David, the shepherd boy who became king, was not only a warrior, but he was also a poet, a writer, a musician, and a dancer (2 Samuel 6:14). He is described as being "the sweet psalmist of Israel" (2 Samuel 23:1) and an inventor of musical instruments (Amos 6:5, 1 Chronicles 23:5). David also wrote at least 73 of the 150 psalms in the Book of Psalms.

    His son, Solomon, also was prolific in writing and music. Besides his contributions to wisdom literature (the books of Ecclesiastes, the

Song of Solomon, and much of Proverbs) he also wrote two psalms (Psalm 72 and 127) and, according to 1 Kings 4:32, "He spake three thousand proverbs: and his songs were a thousand and five." He also "spake of trees, from the cedar tree that is in Lebanon even unto the hyssop that springeth out of the wall: he spake also of beasts, and of fowl, and of creeping things, and of fishes. And there came of all people to hear the wisdom of Solomon, from all kings of the earth, which had heard of his wisdom." (1 Kings 4:33 – 34) If that was not enough, he also made "harps and psalteries for singers: and there were none such seen before in the land of Judah." (2 Chronicles 9:11)

In addition to all these impressive accomplishments in artistic expression by both David and Solomon, David also directed the Levites to appoint musicians to assist with worship. Asaph, the son of Berechiah, along with Heman, Ethan (Jeduthun), and others were appointed to lead worship with singing and "instruments of musick, psalteries and harps and cymbals, sounding, by lifting up the voice with joy." (1 Chronicles 15:16 – 22) Asaph served under both David and Solomon and was also considered a prophet (2 Chronicles 29:30). Years later, his music was still being played under the reign of King Hezekiah. Several of the sons of Asaph, who numbered at least 148 (Nehemiah 7:44), carried on their father's music ministry and were singers (2 Chronicles 5:12).

Not only did these people create a vast array of music, but buried within the superscriptions (titles) of the psalms and the psalms themselves are references to numerous types of instruments, some of which are unknown. For example, in the first verse of Psalms 8, 81, and 84, there is a reference to an "instrument of Gath" (Gittith in the KJV translation). Gath was a Philistine city and the home of the giant Goliath, whom David defeated with a stone and a sling. Other psalms reference flutes (organs in the KJV translation), harps, eight-stringed harps (Psalms 6 and 12, rendered Sheminith in the KJV version), horns, lutes, psalteries (zithers), stringed instruments, timbrels (tambourines), and trumpets. In 2 Samuel 6:5, when the Ark is brought into Jerusalem under David's reign, David and the Israelites "played before the Lord on all manner of instruments made of fir wood, even on harps, and on psalteries, and on timbrels, and on cornets, and on cymbals." Without any musical notation to go with these lyrics (the verses in the Psalms) it is unknown how these tunes sounded.

What is unusual in Scripture is that there are two instruments that seem to be used more often than others when it comes to praise or God taking significant action, especially in times of battle. The first instrument, the harp, was made of wood and used animal intestines for strings. In China, silk was used for strings. Modern harps now use steel, nylon, or carbon fiber but often still use wood for their beck and body.

One place where harps are prevalent is in the Book of Revelation. In Revelation 5:8, just as Jesus is about to open the scroll with seven seals, it states, "And when He had taken the book, the four beasts and four and twenty elders fell down before the Lamb, having every one of them harps, and golden vials full of odours, which are the prayers of saints." Later, when the 144,000 are introduced, there is a song that only they could learn: "And I heard a voice from heaven, as the voice of many waters, and as the voice of a great thunder: and I heard the voice of harpers harping with their harps: And they sung as it were a new song before the throne, and before the four beasts, and the elders: and no man could learn that song but the hundred and forty and four thousand, which were redeemed from the earth." (Revelation 14:2 – 3) The Greek word for harp in these verses is *kithara*, which may imply a lyre. A lyre was a plucked stringed instrument with a rectangular wooden sound box, two arms of uneven length, and a crosspiece on top.

Next, for those that are victorious over the Beast, his image, and his mark, it says, "And I saw another sign in heaven, great and marvellous, seven angels having the seven last plagues; for in them is filled up the wrath of God. And I saw as it were a sea of glass mingled with fire: and them that had gotten the victory over the beast, and over his image, and over his mark, and over the number of his name, stand on the sea of glass, having the harps of God." (Revelation 15:1 – 2) Again, the Greek word here is the same as the other verses. This is in sharp contrast to Psalm 137, where the Israelites who were carried away into the Babylonian exile hung their "harps upon the willows" in mourning. "For there they that carried us away captive required of us a song; and they that wasted us required of us mirth, saying, 'Sing us one of the songs of Zion.'" (Psalm 137:2 – 3) The psalmist then lamented how they could not sing their songs in a foreign land.

Finally, when Babylon is judged in Revelation 18, the production of music will cease. In Revelation 18:22 we learn that "The voice of harpers, and musicians, and of pipers, and trumpeters, shall be heard no more at all in thee; and no craftsman, of whatsoever craft he be, shall be found any more in thee; and the sound of a millstone shall be heard no more at all in thee."

The second instrument that has prominence in Scripture is the trumpet. It makes its appearance in numerous places, including the departure of the Israelites from Sinai, the fall of Jericho, the battle between Gideon and the Midianites (Judges 7), at the rapture, and again in Revelation. Modern trumpets are typically made by starting with a thin sheet of brass. The sheet is then cut into the shape of a horn. The horn is then rolled, welded together, and hammered into shape by hand. From there the instrument is shaped further on a lathe and polished before the valves and other parts are added.

In Numbers 10, God directed Moses to create two silver trumpets for assembling the congregation and for moving the camp. He told Moses to use the trumpets before going into battle (verse nine) and for many other occasions. "Also in the day of your gladness, and in your solemn days, and in the beginnings of your months, ye shall blow with the trumpets over your burnt offerings, and over the sacrifices of your peace offerings; that they may be to you for a memorial before your God: I am the Lord your God." (Numbers 10:10)

God also designated a special day that was referred to as the "Feast of Trumpets" (now called Rosh Hashanah or the beginning of the Jewish New Year). In Leviticus 23:24 – 25 it states, "Speak unto the children of Israel, saying, 'In the seventh month, in the first day of the month, shall ye have a sabbath, a memorial of blowing of trumpets, an holy convocation. Ye shall do no servile work therein: but ye shall offer an offering made by fire unto the Lord.'"

In a similar way, when Joshua entered Canaan God told him that the city of Jericho would be delivered into his hand. The city was encompassed by a wall and none of its inhabitants ventured in or out because of the presence of the Israelites.

> "And ye shall compass the city, all ye men of war, and go round about the city once. Thus shalt thou do six days. And seven priests shall bear before the ark seven trumpets of rams' horns: and the

seventh day ye shall compass the city seven times, and the priests shall blow with the trumpets. And it shall come to pass, that when they make a long blast with the ram's horn, and when ye hear the sound of the trumpet, all the people shall shout with a great shout; and the wall of the city shall fall down flat, and the people shall ascend up every man straight before him." (Joshua 6:3 – 5)

The wall's collapse was not caused by the sound waves from the trumpets or the stomping of feet, but by the power of God. It should be noted here that the Hebrew word for trumpet was *shofar*, which was usually made from a ram's horn.

Continuing the theme of the usage of trumpets by God for significant events, the mysterious and controversial subject of the Rapture includes a reference as does the resurrection of the dead in the End Times. In 1 Thessalonians 4:16 – 17 we find, "For the Lord himself shall descend from heaven with a shout, with the voice of the archangel, and with the trump of God: and the dead in Christ shall rise first: then we which are alive and remain shall be caught up together with them in the clouds, to meet the Lord in the air: and so shall we ever be with the Lord." In 1 Corinthians 15:51 – 52 Paul wrote, "Behold, I shew you a mystery; we shall not all sleep, but we shall all be changed, in a moment, in the twinkling of an eye, at the last trump: for the trumpet shall sound, and the dead shall be raised incorruptible, and we shall be changed."

In Revelation 8 – 11, seven trumpets are sounded from heaven during the judgment of the earth. Each trumpet heralds a new mass cataclysm that ranges from hail and fire (mingled with blood) raining down on the earth to Wormwood arriving to a third of the sun, moon, and stars being struck (Revelation 8:7, 10 – 12). All seven trumpets are sounded by angels, but the seventh trumpet does not sound until after the two witnesses in Revelation 11:1 – 14 have completed their ministry, have been killed, and are then resurrected up to heaven. No time periods are given between the different trumpets, although the two witnesses minister for 1,260 days and are raised from the dead after three-and-a-half days.

What is important to remember with all these examples is not the instruments themselves, but who or what is the object of the songs being played on them and how God responds when praise is directed toward Him. Again, in the case of Jericho, the sound waves from the trumpets did not bring the walls down, it was God Himself. Likewise, there are also parallels between the trumpets used at the fall of Jericho and the seven trumpets of Revelation.

In contrast, there are also some examples in Scripture of instruments being used in a creative yet negative way. This topic will be explored in a later chapter, but for now consider these verses from the Book of Amos, where Amos the prophet confronted those living in Zion and Samaria about their growing passivity toward sin and idolatry:

> "Ye that put far away the evil day, and cause the seat of violence to come near; that lie upon beds of ivory, and stretch themselves upon their couches, and eat the lambs out of the flock, and the calves out of the midst of the stall; that chant to the sound of the viol, and invent to themselves instruments of musick, like David; that drink wine in bowls, and anoint themselves with the chief ointments: but they are not grieved for the affliction of Joseph. Therefore now shall they go captive with the first that go captive, and the banquet of them that stretched themselves shall be removed." (Amos 6:3 – 7)

This brings us to another interesting topic which is the power of praising God. There is an intriguing set of passages in Scripture which talk about King Saul being tormented by a distressing spirit. After the Lord rejected Saul as king, and Samuel the prophet anointed David king over Israel, "the Spirit of the Lord departed from Saul, and an evil spirit from the Lord troubled him." (1 Samuel 16:14) His servants then suggested he "seek out a man, who is a cunning player on an harp: and it shall come to pass, when the evil spirit from God is upon thee, that he shall play with his hand, and thou shalt be well." (1 Samuel 16:16)

One of the servants remembered seeing David being skilled at playing and suggested him to Saul. Saul obliged and sent for David. David arrived and even became Saul's armor bearer. "And it came to pass, when the evil spirit from God was upon Saul, that David took an harp, and played with his hand: so Saul was refreshed, and was well, and the evil spirit departed from him." (1 Samuel 16:23)

Although the friendship between Saul and David began well, it quickly soured. David then killed Golliath, who was tormenting the Israelites, and also grew closer to Saul's son, Jonathan (1 Samuel 18:1). Saul also set David over his men of war (1 Samuel 18:5) and it became the subject of a song.

One day, when David and Saul were returning home, women came out from several towns with "singing and dancing, to meet King Saul, with tabrets, with joy, and with instruments of musick." Only the subject of their song angered Saul. "And the women answered one another as they played, and said, 'Saul hath slain his thousands, and David his ten thousands.'" (1 Samuel 18:6 – 7) This song is brought up by others a few more times.

Saul's attitude changed dramatically after this incident and the next day the distressing spirit returned. In 1 Samuel 18:10, again David played his music for Saul. Saul then flung a spear at David to pin him to the wall but David fled. Despite all this, the Lord was with David. Saul saw that David behaved wisely and was afraid of him (1 Samuel 18:14 – 15). David then married Saul's daughter, Michal, but eventually the distressing spirit returned yet again. In 1 Samuel 19:9, David started playing his music again for Saul but Saul tried to kill him with a spear.

Although this is a large topic on its own, it is clear from these passages that David's music, which was likely praising God, had a spiritual influence on the situation. We are also told elsewhere in Scripture about this concept. For example, in 2 Chronicles 5:13, something remarkable happened when the Ark was brought into Solomon's newly-built temple. "It came even to pass, as the trumpeters and singers were as one, to make one sound to be heard in praising and thanking the Lord; and when they lifted up their voice with the trumpets and cymbals and instruments of musick, and praised the Lord, saying, 'For He is good; for His mercy endureth for ever': that then the house was filled with a cloud, even the house of the Lord."

In James 5:13 we are told, "Is any among you afflicted? Let him pray. Is any merry? Let him sing psalms." In Colossians 3:16, Paul tells us to "Let the word of Christ dwell in you richly in all wisdom; teaching and admonishing one another in psalms and hymns and spiritual songs, singing with grace in your hearts to the Lord."

Gathering the Artists

Likewise, in Acts 16:25, Paul and Silas were in prison yet "sang praises unto God: and the prisoners heard them." A great earthquake followed that shook the prison and opened its doors. Their bonds were also loosed. The keeper of the prison thought the prisoners had fled and so he prepared to kill himself. "But Paul cried with a loud voice, saying, 'Do thyself no harm: for we are all here.'" (Acts 16:28) The jailer then asked, "Sirs, what must I do to be saved?" (Acts 16:30) Paul told him about Jesus Christ and that night the jailer and his household were saved.

Many of the Psalms are hymns of praise, too, and instruct us to praise God. For example, in Psalm 105:2 we are told, "Sing unto Him, sing psalms unto Him: talk ye of all His wondrous works." In Psalm 22:3, David wrote that God "inhabitest the praises of Israel." Even in the Book of Job, through Job's unhelpful friend Elihu, it is implied that God "giveth songs in the night" (Job 35:10).

What if a person does not feel like praising God at a particular moment? I will address this topic more in a later chapter, but even if we do not feel like it, in Psalm 148:3 there are instructions given that read, "Praise ye Him, all His angels: praise ye Him, all His hosts. Praise ye Him, sun and moon: praise Him, all ye stars of light." In Job 38:7, God asks Job where he was when the foundations of the earth were laid and where he was "when the morning stars sang together, and all the sons of God shouted for joy?" There is a subtle implication here that creation itself sings to God, even if an individual believer does not feel like it.

This is an idea Jesus reinforced during His triumphant entry into Jerusalem in the New Testament. "And the multitudes that went before, and that followed, cried, saying, 'Hosanna to the Son of David: Blessed is He that cometh in the name of the Lord; Hosanna in the highest.'" (Matthew 21:9) The Pharisees were angered by this and told Jesus to rebuke His disciples. Jesus replied, "I tell you that, if these should hold their peace, the stones would immediately cry out." (Luke 19:40)

One can only imagine what singing rocks would have sounded like on that day or what the futuristic harps will sound like in heaven. In between these events the possibilities for creativity in the world of music remain vast and full of hope, especially if the music is directed at praising God.

- 7 -

The Image Makers

"And God said, 'Let us make man in Our image, after Our likeness: and let them have dominion over the fish of the sea, and over the fowl of the air, and over the cattle, and over all the earth, and over every creeping thing that creepeth upon the earth.'" – Genesis 1:26

Modern culture is immersed in a world of images. Visual representations exist everywhere from newspapers to cereal boxes, posters to billboards, television to movies, and from smart phones to home computers. Webster's dictionary defines the word "image" several ways, including "a visual representation of something" or an "exact likeness" or even "a mental picture or impression of something". Images can also be captured, such as through a camera, while other images are created, such as through a painting, or they can be strung together to create a movie. Even in the world of technology, one can create an "image" of a computer's hard drive, which is essentially a copy of the all the information stored on it. This can then be used as a backup or to rapidly set up new computer systems at a business.

The Bible also uses this word in both a positive and negative way. As early as the Book of Genesis God states, "And God said, Let Us make man in Our image, after Our likeness: and let them have dominion over the fish of the sea, and over the fowl of the air, and over the cattle, and over all the earth, and over every creeping thing that creepeth upon the earth." (Genesis 1:26) There has been debate for centuries as to whether this created image refers to the physical or the spiritual properties of man, or both. Either way, it was as if God made a "copy" of Himself to a limited extent when He created mankind.

In the New Testament, Paul uses the word *image* in a somewhat different manner. The word he used across all of his letters is the Greek word *eikon*, which means "a likeness". He first uses the word in reference to Jesus in Romans 8:29 where it states, "For whom He did foreknow, He also did predestinate to be conformed to the image of His Son, that He might be the firstborn among many brethren." The first two uses of "he" in this verse refer to God the Father, and it seems to imply an image in a spiritual sense rather than a physical one. Colossians 1:15 also describes Jesus in a similar way, saying that He is "the image of the invisible God, the firstborn of every creature."

At the same time, as believers we are to "put on the new self" as described in Colossians 3:9 – 11, where we are to "Lie not one to another, seeing that ye have put off the old man with his deeds; and have put on the new man, which is renewed in knowledge after the image of Him that created Him: where there is neither Greek nor Jew, circumcision nor uncircumcision, Barbarian, Scythian, bond nor free: but Christ is all, and in all." In 2 Corinthians 3:18 we read, "But we all, with open face beholding as in a glass the glory of the Lord, are changed into the same image from glory to glory, even as by the Spirit of the Lord." Again, both references refer to the spiritual realm rather than the physical one.

This spiritual image is also tied in with the concept of light as found in the discussion of the light of the Gospel and unbelief in 2 Corinthians 4. "But if our gospel be hid, it is hid to them that are lost: in whom the god of this world hath blinded the minds of them which believe not, lest the light of the glorious gospel of Christ, who is the image of God, should shine unto them." (2 Corinthians 4:3 – 4)

In 1 Corinthians 15:1 – 49, Paul discussed the resurrection of Christ but also the resurrection of the dead. He seemed to ultimately link the physical with the spiritual by saying "And as we have borne the image of the earthy, we shall also bear the image of the heavenly." (1 Corinthians 15:49) Perhaps we saw a glimpse of this when Jesus walked the earth in a resurrected body in John 20 – 21.

Despite the wonderful concept of being created in the image of God, like all other things with sinful mankind, it does not take long before corruption sets in. Unfortunately, the same is true of creativity and the arts. Despite an artist's best efforts, it does not take much to turn a sacred concept into a profane one.

In Scripture, the creation of corrupt physical images and idols appears in numerous places along with God's warnings against the practice. Perhaps the most famous warning is found in the Ten Commandments. It is where the concept of the "graven image" comes from. There is also a link between the first and the second commandment as the breaking of the first commandment often leads to the breaking of the second. They read:

> "Thou shalt have no other gods before Me. Thou shalt not make unto thee any graven image, or any likeness of any thing that is in heaven above, or that is in the earth beneath, or that is in the water under the earth: thou shalt not bow down thyself to them, nor serve them: for I the Lord thy God am a jealous God, visiting the iniquity of the fathers upon the children unto the third and fourth generation of them that hate Me; and shewing mercy unto thousands of them that love Me, and keep My commandments." (Exodus 20:3 – 6)

The Hebrew word for "graven image" here is *pesel*, which means a carved or hewn image. This command is repeated again in Leviticus 26:1 and elsewhere.

Why was God so adamant about not making such images and bowing down to them? For the Israelites, several consequences were listed as being possible. God warned them through Moses that the images would be a snare (Deuteronomy 7:25), bring curses (Deuteronomy 27:15), and could even bring about death (Deuteronomy 8:19). Further, in Isaiah 42:8, it was viewed as an attempt to steal glory from God: "I am the Lord: that is My name: and My glory will I not give to another, neither My praise to graven images." In Psalm 78:58, it states that God can be moved to jealousy by them.

Additionally, in the ancient world, the belief that deities could inhabit images and idols was widespread. Because the Israelites came up out of Egypt, which was a land full of images, idols, and various gods, and they were destined to enter a new land with its own set of similar practices (Canaan), Moses gave several commands about the destruction of pagan images. In Deuteronomy 7:5 the Israelites were told to "Destroy their altars, and break down their images, and cut down their groves, and burn their graven images with fire." Numbers 33:52 mentioned they were to "destroy all their pictures" and Deuteronomy 12:3 adds they should "hew down the graven images of their gods, and destroy the names of them out of that place." For a replacement altar, in Deuteronomy 16:21 – 22 Moses went further and stated, "Thou shalt not plant thee a grove of any trees near unto the altar of the Lord thy God, which thou shalt make thee. Neither shalt thou set thee up any image; which the Lord thy God hateth."

Does this mean that all artwork made in the "likeness of any thing that is in heaven above, or that is in the earth beneath, or that is in the water under the earth" is forbidden? As discussed earlier, images of cherubim were commanded to be incorporated into the curtains of the tabernacle. Carvings of cherubim were also commanded to be placed on top of the Ark of the Covenant. In Ezekiel's temple vision, he saw images of palm trees and cherubim on the walls and posts.

The snare seems to occur when the image becomes the center of worship. Regardless of whether the image is religious or not, there could be unintended consequences depending upon the viewer. What one person ignores or views as just a piece of art could turn into an unintended object of worship for another. In some cases, an artist could even cause others to stumble because of it. For example, Paul states in 1 Corinthians 8:9 that believers should "take heed lest by any means this liberty of yours become a stumblingblock to them that are weak." Even though he was discussing eating foods sacrificed to idols, the concept could just as easily be applied to images.

In the case of the nation of Israel, from the time they left Egypt through the return from exile, images were indeed a snare to them. Those images brought curses, death, and judgment. After Solomon died, the nation split into two kingdoms: the tribe of Judah under the reign of Solomon's son Rehoboam and the remaining tribes under Jeroboam I. Both kingdoms struggled under a series of kings, some of which followed the Lord while others did not. Of the kings that did not follow the Lord, they led their people into idolatry and into the worship of foreign gods. Although each kingdom took their own route, both ended up being removed from the land by foreign armies (Israel by Assyria and Judah by Babylon).

For Judah, the decline began under King Rehoboam. In 1 Kings 14:22 – 23 we read, "And Judah did evil in the sight of the Lord, and they provoked Him to jealousy with their sins which they had committed, above all that their fathers had done. For they also built them high places, and images, and groves, on every high hill, and under every green tree." Following Rehoboam, his son Abijah took the throne but in 1 Kings 15:3 – 4 it states, "He walked in all the sins of his father, which he had done before him: and his heart was not perfect with the Lord his God, as the heart of David his father. Nevertheless for David's sake did the Lord his God give him a lamp in Jerusalem, to set up his son after him, and to establish Jerusalem."

After Abijah, the pattern reversed under King Asa (1 Kings 15:9 – 24) and although he did what was right in the eyes of God, he did not remove the high places that were previously built. This back-and-forth trend continued under each new king with mixed results until King Hezekiah.

King Hezekiah undertook many reforms and the people "brake the images in pieces, and cut down the groves, and threw down the high places and the altars out of all Judah and Benjamin, in Ephraim also and Manasseh, until they had utterly destroyed them all." (2 Chronicles 31:1) He also did "that which was good and right and truth before the Lord his God" (2 Chronicles 31:20) and after humbling himself before the Lord, the Lord even extended his life.

By the time his successor took over, God's overall patience ran out. King Manasseh took the throne at the age of twelve and reigned fifty-five years. He did the opposite of Hezekiah and he "built up again the high places which Hezekiah his father had destroyed; and he reared up altars for Baal, and made a grove, as did Ahab king of Israel; and worshipped all the host of heaven, and served them." (2 Kings 21:3) Then, his idolatry took a more ominous turn. "And he built altars in the house of the Lord, of which the Lord said, 'In Jerusalem will I put my name.' And he built altars for all the host of heaven in the two courts of the house of the Lord." (2 Kings 21:4 – 5)

As a result, he "made his son pass through the fire, and observed times, and used enchantments, and dealt with familiar spirits and wizards: he wrought much wickedness in the sight of the Lord, to provoke Him to anger. And he set a graven image of the grove that he had made in the house, of which the Lord said to David, and to

Gathering the Artists

Solomon his son, 'In this house, and in Jerusalem, which I have chosen out of all tribes of Israel, will I put my name for ever.'" (2 Kings 21:6 – 7) The people also followed his example because he "seduced them to do more evil than did the nations whom the Lord destroyed before the children of Israel." (2 Kings 21:9) He also shed much innocent blood (2 Kings 21:16).

These acts in the eyes of God were the final straw. King Manasseh was *even worse* than the Canaanites that were driven out of the Promised Land and he took an entire nation with him. At this point God announced His judgment on Judah, but the actual enforcement did not occur immediately. After Manasseh's reign, his son Amon took over, but he, too, followed in the footsteps of his father. His reign lasted two years until he was killed in his own house by his servants. His son, Josiah, then took the throne.

Josiah was eight years old when he became king and reigned thirty-one years. Yet God stayed His judgment during this time. Hilkiah, a high priest, rediscovered the Book of the Law and when it was read to the king, the king tore his clothes. The Lord then told him:

"Because thine heart was tender, and thou hast humbled thyself before the Lord, when thou heardest what I spake against this place, and against the inhabitants thereof, that they should become a desolation and a curse, and hast rent thy clothes, and wept before Me; I also have heard thee, saith the Lord. Behold therefore, I will gather thee unto thy fathers, and thou shalt be gathered into thy grave in peace; and thine eyes shall not see all the evil which I will bring upon this place." (2 Kings 22:19 – 20)

Josiah then instituted numerous reforms as listed in 2 Kings 23:1 – 27. He burned the vessels that were devoted to Baal (verse four), put down the idolatrous priests who "burned incense unto Baal, to the sun, and to the moon, and to the planets, and to all the host of heaven" (verse five), burned their images (verse six), and broke down houses nearby that had weavings devoted to the images (verse seven). He defiled a place devoted to child sacrifice, Topheth, which was dedicated to Molech (verse 10), took away horses that were dedicated to the sun (verse 11), burned their chariots, and destroyed other altars (verse 12). He also defiled the high places devoted to Ashtoreth, Chemosh, and Milcom (verse 13).

From these verses, it is clear to see that Judah did not just fall into image worship of a single god. Instead they adopted the images, idols, and practices of many. After Josiah died the final judgment came and the people were carried away to Babylon (2 Kings 25:1 – 21).

It is sobering to contemplate how images can influence the course of a nation. For those involved in their creation, even greater thought must be put into the potential impacts. What's more, the internet and broadcast media have become so pervasive that a single image (as a picture) can circle the world in seconds. It can then be copied an endless number of times with minimal effort on the part of an individual. It's incredible to think that an image that an artist creates could impact people separated by thousands of miles without ever having to meet face-to-face. It is also daunting to think of the amount and type of images that our modern culture is bombarded with on a daily basis. Where will these images lead us?

- 8 -

The Idol Makers

"Wherefore, my dearly beloved, flee from idolatry." – 1 Corinthians 10:14

What, exactly, is an idol? According to the *Zondervan Encyclopedia of the Bible*, in ancient times it was believed "that the image was the dwelling place of a superhuman force of being, or was the deity itself. Idols were made of wood, stone, or clay, and sometimes of gold or silver." (Zondervan, Volume 3, 270) Often sheets of beaten silver or gold were spread over wood or stone (Isaiah 40:19 – 20) or the idol was made of a precious metal and left hollow. Another definition of the word is found in Webster's Dictionary, which describes it as "an object of extreme devotion".

Like images in the previous chapter, the creation and worship of idols represented a breaking of both the first and second of the Ten Commandments. In the Old and New Testaments, God repeatedly warned us not to become involved with it. In Exodus 34:17 it reads, "Thou shalt make thee no molten gods" while in 1 John 5:21 it warns, "Little children, keep yourselves from idols." In Galatians 5:20, Paul lists idolatry as a work of the flesh and we are to flee from it (1 Corinthians 10:14).

Why should we flee? In Exodus 34:14, God told the Israelites, "For thou shalt worship no other god: for the Lord, whose name is Jealous, is a jealous God." In Hosea 13:4, God says "There is no Saviour beside Me" and again in Isaiah 43:11 it states that "I, even I, am the Lord; and beside Me there is no saviour."

So why do people do create idols anyway? With the Israelites, it often started with unbelief. They also hardened their necks (and hearts) toward God. In 2 Kings 17:15 – 17 we read:

> "And they rejected His statutes, and His covenant that He made with their fathers, and His testimonies which He testified against them; and they followed vanity, and became vain, and went after the heathen that were round about them, concerning whom the Lord had charged them, that they should not do like them. And they left all the commandments of the Lord their God, and made them molten images, even two calves, and made a grove, and worshipped all the host of heaven, and served Baal. And they caused their sons and their daughters to pass through the fire, and used divination and enchantments, and sold themselves to do evil in the sight of the Lord, to provoke Him to anger."

In Romans 1:18 – 32, Paul also referenced unbelief. Despite God's revelation through creation and via other means, unrighteous people knowingly suppress the truth (verse 18), do not glorify God, and are unthankful for Him (verse 21). This leads to vanity (verse 21), foolishness (verse 22), and the replacing of God's glory with corruptible idols (verse 23).

As a result, God turns them over to uncleanness and dishonor (verse 24), vile affections (verse 26), and a long list of other practices which ultimately lead to death (verses 28 – 32). As a whole, it is about exchanging the truth of God for a lie. It is also about worshipping and serving "the creature more than the Creator." (verse 25)

In the previous chapter, the consequences for Judah and Israel's image worship were discussed. For idols (which are sometimes interchangeable with images), the list is even longer. First, with idols that are statues, they do not speak, must be carried, and do not actually do anything physical (Jeremiah 10:2 – 5). They are mute, cannot teach, and have no breath in them at all (Habakkuk 2:18 – 19). They cannot save (Hosea 13:4), are wind and confusion (Isaiah 41:29), and ultimately will perish because they are of this earth (Jeremiah 10:11).

Like images, idols can bring curses (Deuteronomy 27:15), can be a snare (Psalm 106:36), and can lead to shame and fear (Isaiah 44:9 –

11, Psalm 97:7). In Isaiah 2:8, it states they also lead to self-worship. In Hosea 9:10, because of idol worship, the Israelites fell into shame and "their abominations were according as they loved." Even in the End Times, as described in the Book of Revelation, unbelief and idol worship leads to a lack of repentance despite mass cataclysms occurring on earth. "And the rest of the men which were not killed by these plagues yet repented not of the works of their hands, that they should not worship devils, and idols of gold, and silver, and brass, and stone, and of wood: which neither can see, nor hear, nor walk: neither repented they of their murders, nor of their sorceries, nor of their fornication, nor of their thefts." (Revelation 9:20 – 21)

Impatience with God also seems to be another pathway to idol worship. The most prominent example was when Moses was about to walk down off Mount Sinai after spending forty days and forty nights communing and conversing with God (Exodus 32:1 – 35). The Israelites, even though they knew where Moses was and saw the cloud covering the mountain, told Aaron, "Up, make us gods, which shall go before us; for as for this Moses, the man that brought us up out of the land of Egypt, we wot not what is become of him." (verse one) Aaron then directed them to break off their golden earrings, melted them together in a fire, and engraved the end result. He then declared, "These be thy gods, O Israel, which brought thee up out of the land of Egypt." (verse four)

Then he built an altar for it and strangely declared the following day would be a feast unto the Lord (verse five). God spoke to Moses about what they did and said, "Now therefore let Me alone, that My wrath may wax hot against them, and that I may consume them: and I will make of thee a great nation." (verse 10) Moses pleaded with God not to destroy them. God relented and Moses descended down the mountain.

When he arrived back at camp, he saw the Israelites dancing before the golden calf. Incensed, he smashed the tablets that contained the Ten Commandments (verses 15 – 19). "And he took the calf which they had made, and burnt it in the fire, and ground it to powder, and strawed it upon the water, and made the children of Israel drink of it." (verse 20) He then confronted Aaron. Aaron explained what happened, but also altered the details of the story. He claimed he cast the earrings "into the fire, and there came out this calf." (verse 24)

Gathering the Artists

Aaron also had told the people to go naked (verse 25).

Then Moses called those who believed in the Lord to himself. All of the sons of Levi came to his side and he said, "Thus saith the Lord God of Israel, 'Put every man his sword by his side, and go in and out from gate to gate throughout the camp, and slay every man his brother, and every man his companion, and every man his neighbour.'" (verse 27) Three thousand died that day and the Lord plagued others in the camp afterward (verses 28 – 35).

The golden calf idol reappeared again under the reign of Jeroboam I during his rebellion against Rehoboam, king of Judah. In order to keep his people from heading to Jerusalem to worship at God's temple, he "took counsel, and made two calves of gold, and said unto them, 'It is too much for you to go up to Jerusalem: behold thy gods, O Israel, which brought thee up out of the land of Egypt.'" (1 Kings 12:28) Just like Aaron, he also ordained a feast "in the eighth month, on the fifteenth day of the month, like unto the feast that is in Judah, and he offered upon the altar. So did he in Bethel, sacrificing unto the calves that he had made: and he placed in Bethel the priests of the high places which he had made." (1 Kings 12:32)

There is also a hint in Scripture that impatience with God will abound during the End Times. In 2 Peter 3:3 – 4, in reference to Jesus' second coming, Peter warns, "Knowing this first, that there shall come in the last days scoffers, walking after their own lusts, and saying, 'Where is the promise of His coming? For since the fathers fell asleep, all things continue as they were from the beginning of the creation.'" As we will see shortly, idol worship will be prominent in the end of days and this could be the pathway to it.

Before we leave the subject of Moses and the idolatry of the people he led through the wilderness, there is another curious incident found in Numbers 21. As the Israelites travelled in the wilderness toward the Promised Land, they complained. "Wherefore have ye brought us up out of Egypt to die in the wilderness? For there is no bread, neither is there any water; and our soul loatheth this light bread." (Numbers 21:5) The Lord's response was to send "fiery serpents" among the people until they begged Moses to intercede for them. The Lord told Moses, "Make thee a fiery serpent, and set it upon a pole: and it shall come to pass, that every one that is bitten, when he looketh upon it, shall live." (Numbers 21:8)

Those who gazed upon the bronze serpent on the pole lived. King Hezekiah destroyed the object in his day, though, because the people turned it into an idol, burned incense to it, and called it "Nehushtan" (2 Kings 18:4) In the New Testament, Jesus referred back to the object's original purpose as a reference to Himself. "And as Moses lifted up the serpent in the wilderness, even so must the Son of Man be lifted up: that whosoever believeth in Him should not perish, but have eternal life." (John 3:14 – 15)

A final example of physical idolatry to consider is found in the Book of Daniel. Daniel and his friends were carried off during the exile to Babylon. They believed in God and honored Him with their words and actions despite the culture that stood in opposition to them. God even gave Daniel the ability to interpret King Nebuchadnezzar's dream, since his magicians, astrologers, sorcerers, and the Chaldeans could not (Daniel 2:1 – 45). Daniel was then promoted, and he was able to secure new positions for his friends in the government (Daniel 2:49).

Then the king "made an image of gold, whose height was threescore cubits, and the breadth thereof six cubits: he set it up in the plain of Dura, in the province of Babylon." (Daniel 3:1) The king gathered many leaders and judges together for a dedication ceremony. A herald announced, "To you it is commanded, O people, nations, and languages, that at what time ye hear the sound of the cornet, flute, harp, sackbut, psaltery, dulcimer, and all kinds of musick, ye fall down and worship the golden image that Nebuchadnezzar the king hath set up: and whoso falleth not down and worshippeth shall the same hour be cast into the midst of a burning fiery furnace." (Daniel 3:4 – 6) Then, "certain Chaldeans came near, and accused the Jews." (Daniel 3:8)

Daniel's friends, Shadrach, Meshach, and Abednego, refused to bow down and worship the giant golden image. They were brought before the king and he interrogated them under the threat of throwing them into the fiery furnace. They replied, "O Nebuchadnezzar, we are not careful to answer thee in this matter. If it be so, our God whom we serve is able to deliver us from the burning fiery furnace, and He will deliver us out of thine hand, O king. But if not, be it known unto thee, O king, that we will not serve thy gods, nor worship the golden image which thou hast set up." (Daniel 3:16 – 18)

The king was enraged. He commanded that the furnace be made seven times hotter than normal and that Daniel's friends be bound and thrown into the fire. Because the request was urgent and the furnace abnormally hot, the fire ended up killing the men who threw his friends into the fire (Daniel 3:19 – 22).

Astonished, the king said to his counselors, "Lo, I see four men loose, walking in the midst of the fire, and they have no hurt; and the form of the fourth is like the Son of God." (Daniel 3:25). He called them out of the fire yet not a "hair of their head singed, neither were their coats changed, nor the smell of fire had passed on them." (Daniel 3:27) The king then praised God and decreed that anybody that spoke against their God would "be cut in pieces, and their houses shall be made a dunghill: because there is no other God that can deliver after this sort." (Daniel 3:29)

There are eerie parallels between this incident and the idol worship found in the Book of Revelation. Two beasts appear in chapter thirteen, one from the sea and another from the earth. The first beast receives a mortal wound but is healed. The second beast then causes everyone to worship the first beast, "and he doeth great wonders, so that he maketh fire come down from heaven on the earth in the sight of men, and deceiveth them that dwell on the earth by the means of those miracles which he had power to do in the sight of the beast; saying to them that dwell on the earth, that they should make an image to the beast, which had the wound by a sword, and did live. And he had power to give life unto the image of the beast, that the image of the beast should both speak, and cause that as many as would not worship the image of the beast should be killed." (Revelation 13:13 – 15)

This is then followed by proclamations from three angels, the third of which announces:

"If any man worship the beast and his image, and receive his mark in his forehead, or in his hand, the same shall drink of the wine of the wrath of God, which is poured out without mixture into the cup of his indignation; and he shall be tormented with fire and brimstone in the presence of the holy angels, and in the presence of the Lamb: and the smoke of their torment ascendeth up for ever and ever: and they have no rest day nor night, who worship the beast and his image, and whosoever receiveth the mark of his name." (Revelation 14:9 – 11)

When the seven bowl (vial) judgments arrive in Revelation 16, the first one is directed at the worshippers of the image. In Revelation 16:2 it reads, "And the first went, and poured out his vial upon the earth; and there fell a noisome and grievous sore upon the men which had the mark of the beast, and upon them which worshipped his image." Yet for those who do not worship the beast or its image, "they lived and reigned with Christ a thousand years." (Revelation 20:4)

All these references to idols and their destructive power leads to another question: do idols have to be physical objects? According to Colossians 3:5, covetousness is also idolatry. In Ezekiel 14, while Ezekiel the prophet was in exile in Babylon, he was approached by some elders of Israel. Before they even spoke, God told the prophet that "these men have set up their idols in their heart, and put the stumblingblock of their iniquity before their face: should I be enquired of at all by them?" (Ezekiel 14:3) The "idols in their hearts" caused estrangement from God. God then told Ezekiel that anybody harboring these idols would cause Him to set His "face against that man" and that He would "make him a sign and a proverb" and "cut him off from the midst of my people; and ye shall know that I am the Lord". (Ezekiel 14:8) Even though there may not have been any physical manifestation of idolatry to Ezekiel, God could see that it existed in their hearts.

If idols can exist both as physical objects and in the heart, and if idols can be works of art, could creativity itself ever become an idol? The act of creation can be invigorating. It can also be intoxicating. In some mediums, it can lead an artist into realms that other artists have rarely explored or have not explored successfully.

Creativity can also be an act of worship and that worship can be directed either at God, oneself, or something else. Probably the ultimate example of creativity (and engineering) becoming an idol can be found in Genesis 11:1 – 9. The Tower of Babel was built of bricks and asphalt on a plain in the land of Shinar (verses 2 – 3). It was also built during a time when the whole earth used a single language (verse one). "And they said, Go to, let us build us a city and a tower, whose top may reach unto heaven; and let us make us a name, lest we be scattered abroad upon the face of the whole earth." (Genesis 11:4) Although no physical description of the tower is given, its purpose was self-glorification.

The Lord responded, "Behold, the people is one, and they have all one language; and this they begin to do: and now nothing will be restrained from them, which they have imagined to do. Go to, let Us go down, and there confound their language, that they may not understand one another's speech." (Genesis 11:6 – 7) He then scattered the people and construction ceased (verse eight).

This confusion of languages was reversed somewhat at Pentecost. In Acts 2:1 – 39, the disciples gathered together and received the Holy Spirit and "began to speak with other tongues, as the Spirit gave them utterance." (Acts 2:4) Men were gathered there from "every nation under heaven" (verse five) and "were confounded, because that every man heard them speak in his own language." (verse six) Paul later explained that the ability to speak in tongues and interpret those tongues was a gift of the Holy Spirit (1 Corinthians 12:10, 1 Corinthians 12:28, and elsewhere).

At the Tower of Babel, the glorification of man (and self) led to judgment and division. At Pentecost, the glorification of God led to honor and unity, but in an unexpected way. If you ever created art in the past, who or what did it glorify? Not every piece of art is intended to glorify a spiritual being but most art museums will usually have something on display that does connect on a spiritual level. And, just like images, idols have the potential to lead entire nations astray.

- 9 -

The Critics

"For the preaching of the cross is to them that perish foolishness; but unto us which are saved it is the power of God." – 1 Corinthians 1:18

Are you a creative person? Do you like to draw, paint, write, sculpt, dance, work with fabric, make films, play music, or create art in other mediums? Have you tried to combine that passion and gift with faith? What happened?

If your experience even remotely matches mine, two things probably happened simultaneously. On one hand there was joy in the act of creation and a sense of deep fulfillment. At the same time, if you shared the resulting art with someone else it was either met with similar joy or great opposition.

When an artist puts their heart into their work they give a piece of themselves away in the process. When that art is then given away to the world it is subject to interpretation. As a result, the artist may be extra sensitive to any criticism of their work, however fair or unfair that criticism is. Yet when faith is intertwined with the art, not only is the work more personal for the artist, but it is also judged differently by the recipient. When it comes to religious matters in general, the debate often involves intense emotions on both sides and in some situations it can even get hostile.

What sometimes follows for an artist of faith is a sense of depression and questioning whether God *really* called them to create in the first place. It does not help that depression is not a popular subject in many churches today. There can sometimes be multiple causes of depression and it can come from emotional, physical, psychological, spiritual, or medical issues. Regardless of the cause, some feel that Christians are supposed to be filled with joy anyway and if you are experiencing depression it must be because *you* are the problem or *you* are doing something wrong. Nothing could be further from the truth. As an artist, it can also mean you are doing something *right*.

Examples of depression can be found throughout the Bible as well as how many heroes of the faith dealt with it. In Genesis 37:3, we learn that Jacob "loved Joseph more than all his children, because he was the son of his old age: and he made him a coat of many colours." This provoked Joseph's brothers to hate him, and subsequently God gave Joseph a dream about his brother's sheaves in the field bowing down to his sheaf. The interpretation was that one day his brothers would bow down to him (Genesis 37:7). That dream was followed by another dream where the sun, the moon, and eleven stars were in obedience to him (Genesis 37:9), where again it symbolized his brothers bowing down to him.

His brothers then conspired to kill him, but Reuben (one of his brothers) intervened and convinced them instead to have Joseph thrown into a pit. They were then approached by a group of Midianite traders and sold Joseph into slavery for twenty pieces of silver (Genesis 37:18 – 28). Then his brothers "took Joseph's coat, and killed a kid of the goats, and dipped the coat in the blood." (Genesis 37:31) They sent the coat of many colors back to Jacob who mourned over the loss of his son.

The rest of the story is that Joseph rose to prominence in Egypt by God's provision, despite being thrown in jail and being accused of hitting on Potiphar's wife (Genesis 39). He then was forgotten by his fellow prisoners despite interpreting their dreams (Genesis 40). He eventually was allowed to interpret Potiphar's dreams and rose to power due to God having favor upon him (Genesis 41). In the midst of a famine, his brothers then returned along with their father. Joseph provided food for them and, as foretold in his dreams, they became subservient to him (Genesis 42 – 47). When they finally did bow down to him, he declared "But as for you, ye thought evil against me; but God meant it unto good, to bring to pass, as it is this day, to save much people alive." (Genesis 50:20)

Moses and Jeremiah also went through periods of depression. Ezra the priest and Nehemiah battled opposition in the form of harassing letters and scoffers during the rebuilding of the second temple and the walls around Jerusalem. What was Nehemiah's response? He turned his oppressors over to God and asked, "Now therefore, O God, strengthen my hands." (Nehemiah 6:9)

David also dealt with depression. While on the run and hiding in caves from King Saul, David wrote Psalm 57 and Psalm 142. He cried out to God, "Be merciful unto me, O God, be merciful unto me: for my soul trusteth in thee: yea, in the shadow of thy wings will I make my refuge, until these calamities be overpast." (Psalm 57:1) In verse four he laments, "My soul is among lions: and I lie even among them that are set on fire, even the sons of men, whose teeth are spears and arrows, and their tongue a sharp sword." Yet throughout the psalm David found a way to praise God.

In Psalm 142:4, David wrote, "I looked on my right hand, and beheld, but there was no man that would know me: refuge failed me; no man cared for my soul." In verse six he wrote, "Attend unto my cry; for I am brought very low: deliver me from my persecutors; for they are stronger than I." In both psalms, David directed his anxiety toward the Lord despite being depressed and feeling alone even though he was surrounded by others.

Elijah, too, was familiar with depression. After his dramatic defeat of the prophets of Baal on Mount Carmel in 1 Kings 18:1 – 46, he fled into the wilderness. Word got back to King Ahab's wife, Jezebel, and he felt his life was in danger. Then, he "went a day's journey into the wilderness, and came and sat down under a juniper tree: and he requested for himself that he might die; and said, 'It is enough; now, O Lord, take away my life; for I am not better than my fathers.'" (1 Kings 19:4) He fell asleep under the tree until an angel arrived and told him, "Arise and eat." (1 Kings 19:5)

When he awoke, he found a cake baked on coals and a jug of water (1 Kings 19:6). He ate and then went back asleep. A second angel arrived and told him "arise and eat" again "because the journey is too great for thee." (1 Kings 19:7) He then traveled to Mount Horeb where the Lord spoke to him while he hid in a cave. The Lord asked him, "What doest thou here, Elijah?" (1 Kings 19:9) Elijah's reply was one of deep depression. "I have been very jealous for the Lord God of hosts: for the children of Israel have forsaken thy covenant, thrown down thine altars, and slain thy prophets with the sword; and I, even I only, am left; and they seek my life, to take it away." (1 Kings 19:10)

God then called Elijah out of the cave and told him to stand outside. The Lord passed by, and a great wind shook the mountains and broke rocks. Then came an earthquake and finally a fire. "But the Lord was not in the fire: and after the fire a still small voice." (1 Kings 19:11 – 12) Again, God asked him what he was doing there. Elijah repeated his earlier lament. God then told him to return on his way to Damascus, anoint Hazael king in Syria, anoint Jehu to be king of Israel, and to then anoint Elisha as his successor. Perhaps the tenderest moment came when God gave Elijah some perspective and told him he was not alone by saying, "Yet I have left Me seven thousand in Israel, all the knees which have not bowed unto Baal, and every mouth which hath not kissed him." (1 Kings 19:18)

Even Jonah the prophet dealt with depression, although he was a curious example because there was no apparent opposition to his message. In Jonah 4:3, after Jonah finally followed God's command to deliver a call to repentance to the Gentile city of Nineveh, Jonah cried out in his anger, "Therefore now, O Lord, take, I beseech thee, my life from me; for it is better for me to die than to live." Jonah was angry with God for sparing the wicked city of Nineveh, even though Nineveh repented immediately at Jonah's preaching.

God then replied, "Doest thou well to be angry?" (Jonah 4:4) Jonah then went and sat east of the city and waited for its potential demise. God then prepared a plant (gourd) to grow over Jonah's head to protect him from the heat of the sun. A day later God prepared a worm to destroy the plant.

Jonah then repeated his request to die. God again challenged his angry feelings and gave the prophet some much needed perspective. "Then said the Lord, 'Thou hast had pity on the gourd, for the which thou hast not laboured, neither madest it grow; which came up in a night, and perished in a night: and should not I spare Nineveh, that great city, wherein are more than sixscore thousand persons that cannot discern between their right hand and their left hand; and also much cattle?'" (Jonah 4:10 – 11)

If these Biblical figures did God's will, albeit sometimes reluctantly, why did they get depressed and why did some encounter so much opposition to their efforts? Some opposition was borne out of human nature but the rest was probably not of this world.

This concept is spelled out in Ephesians 6:12, where Paul wrote, "For we wrestle not against flesh and blood, but against principalities, against powers, against the rulers of the darkness of this world, against spiritual wickedness in high places." Ephesians 6 is where Paul also described how to counter such opposition and that the weapons are provided solely by God. In 2 Corinthians 4:3 – 4, Paul also counseled, "But if our gospel be hid, it is hid to them that are lost: in whom the god of this world hath blinded the minds of them which believe not, lest the light of the glorious gospel of Christ, who is the image of God, should shine unto them."

Paul encountered this principle numerous times as described throughout his letters in the New Testament. One of the more prominent examples is found in Acts 19:21 – 41, where his preaching in Ephesus triggered a riot. In verses 23 – 25 it reads, "And the same time there arose no small stir about that Way. For a certain man named Demetrius, a silversmith, which made silver shrines for Diana, brought no small gain unto the craftsmen; whom he called together with the workmen of like occupation, and said, 'Sirs, ye know that by this craft we have our wealth.'" Demetrius then stirred up the workers by condemning Paul's preaching, stated their trade was in danger, and that Diana would be "despised".

The angry crowd then seized Paul's companions and his disciples held him back from confronting the crowd. A city clerk intervened and was able to reason with the crowd and got them to back down. Was this incident only about a loss of income?

Sometimes opposition that a faith-based artist encounters is just a flat-out spiritual attack. It can be difficult to sort out what is constructive criticism and what is an attack, which is why prayer and the trusted counsel of others can be so important. Like any other piece of art, it is best to put your "best foot forward" and hone your craft at every opportunity so that the focus is not on the quality of the implementation but rather the content. A helpful discussion of these concepts can be found in Chip Ingram's book, *The Invisible War*. It is a fantastic Biblically-grounded overview of the issue of spiritual warfare and offers sound practical advice for dealing with it.

Scripture is also replete with verses that speak to the suffering, trials, and persecution that a Christian will endure. Some trials have a specific purpose as explained in James 1:2 – 4: "My brethren, count it all joy when ye fall into divers temptations; knowing this, that the trying of your faith worketh patience. But let patience have her perfect work, that ye may be perfect and entire, wanting nothing." 1 Peter 4:12 – 13 states, "Beloved, think it not strange concerning the fiery trial which is to try you, as though some strange thing happened unto you: but rejoice, inasmuch as ye are partakers of Christ's sufferings; that, when His glory shall be revealed, ye may be glad also with exceeding joy." Paul wrote in 2 Timothy 3:12, "Yea, and all that will live godly in Christ Jesus shall suffer persecution." Jesus also said, "Blessed are ye, when men shall revile you, and persecute you, and shall say all manner of evil against you falsely, for My sake. Rejoice, and be exceeding glad: for great is your reward in heaven: for so persecuted they the prophets which were before you." (Matthew 5:12 – 13)

Peter also talked about a different kind of suffering as a Christian, not because of external persecution but because of one's own sins. "But let none of you suffer as a murderer, or as a thief, or as an evildoer, or as a busybody in other men's matters. Yet if any man suffer as a Christian, let him not be ashamed; but let him glorify God on this behalf. For the time is come that judgment must begin at the house of God: and if it first begin at us, what shall the end be of them that obey not the gospel of God?" (1 Peter 4:15 – 17)

There is also a warning in Scripture about being a teacher. James said, "My brethren, be not many masters, knowing that we shall receive the greater condemnation." (James 3:1) In the NKJV, "masters" is rendered as "teachers" and "greater condemnation" as "stricter judgment". In other words, if you are a teacher of the Word, or perhaps an artist who incorporates the Word into your art, God will hold you to a higher standard.

Remember, Jesus is the "stone the builders rejected" (Acts 4:11, Matthew 21:42, and elsewhere) and He is also the "great high priest, that is passed into the heavens" and "We have not an high priest which cannot be touched with the feeling of our infirmities; but was in all points tempted like as we are, yet without sin." (Hebrews 4:14 – 15) Hebrews 13:5 also adds, "Let your conversation be without covetousness; and be content with such things as ye have: for He hath said, I will never leave thee, nor forsake thee."

As an artist, it is also important to avoid falling into a comparison trap. Paul wrote in 1 Corinthians 3:6 – 9, "I have planted, Apollos watered; but God gave the increase. So then neither is he that planteth any thing, neither he that watereth; but God that giveth the increase. Now he that planteth and he that watereth are one: and every man shall receive his own reward according to his own labour. For we are labourers together with God: ye are God's husbandry, ye are God's building."

Lastly, I want to mention something I experienced while writing the science fiction book, *Theft at the Speed of Light*. To this day, that particular book was one of the weirdest and most difficult manuscripts to write. It is about a software engineer who works at a company that designs tracking chips. He becomes caught between an advocacy group that believes the fulfillment of the "mark of the Beast" is at hand (Revelation 13) and a company client who seems intent on pursuing technology that may indeed be a precursor to fulfilling such a prophecy. It was a topic that bothered me for a while and I worked on the book inconsistently over a fifteen year period. As a result, it went through four very different iterations. Despite my unhappiness with parts of the story, even after I considered it "done", at some point I had to just stop tinkering with it.

It was also a manuscript where God showed up in a significant way. During the writing of one version of it, I struggled to make any progress. So I simply asked God one day what was interfering with my writing. At the time I was a big coffee drinker and some days I would drink at least a pot-and-a-half of the black stuff. Like many others, I loved coffee shops, too.

Something unusual happened after that prayer and I did not put all the pieces together until a few weeks later. I had tried to quit drinking coffee months earlier but that only lasted two weeks. A few days before the prayer the coffee at my workplace started to taste strange. I thought it was just me or someone was not making coffee right in the break room.

The following day after the prayer, as I was reaching for a coffee pot, it dawned on me. The coffee was causing the problems. I switched off the coffee pot and only had four or five more cups in the following month before completely ending my coffee drinking for good.

Here is where it gets interesting. After the prayer, every cup of coffee tasted strange. I thought again that it was just some bad break room coffee, so I got the "good stuff", in the form of a cup of Starbucks coffee. I tasted it once and it ended up sitting on my desk until I threw it out. I completely lost my taste for it. In fact, the final cup of coffee actually made me sick after only a few sips.

Then, there were the scenes in the novel I wanted to toss out. For instance, there is a scene where the main character picks up a penny in his driveway and reads the words "In God We Trust" that is spelled out across the top of the coin. Even though the book deals with financial issues and what it might be like to transition to a cashless society, I thought to myself, "This is unnecessary. It doesn't add anything to the story."

The following day I attended a Bible study at a local church. There on the table in the room where we held our study was a lone penny. Finding it unusual, I asked someone why it was there. They replied, "Some people were discussing earlier about how people want to take the words "In God We Trust" off of our money."

So I left the scene in.

Then, there was a scene where the main character walks into a church and sees a man writing in a little notebook before the service starts. Again I thought, "This is unnecessary. Who does that anyway?" In yet another Bible study, someone mentioned how they bring a little notebook with them to church and take notes on sermons.

So I left that scene in, too.

One of the more unusual things that occurred as I worked on the third iteration of the novel relates to the title. *The title is not mine.* For years the manuscript had no title and the ideas I had for it were junk. So I tried something different and prayed about it. The answer I got back (almost immediately) was the phrase "theft at the speed of light". At first I thought, "No, that's no good. That won't work. It doesn't even fit the story." As the third iteration of the manuscript morphed into the fourth iteration, the story seemed to grow "into" the title. So I left it alone.

The other major problem with the novel was my antipathy and general uneasiness toward the subject in general. As a writer, sometimes it is easy when an idea first comes to you to write quickly and remain energized about it. Over time, especially if the implementation drags out over a period of years, that energy wanes. In the case of this particular book, it ground to a halt multiple times.

A funny thing started to happen every time I got to the point of giving up. Discussions about the Book of Jonah started to pop up. It came in the form of sermons, books, radio broadcasts, television shows, and even random church sermons. I even remember ice fishing up in the middle of nowhere on Lake of the Woods and listening to a transistor radio for about a half hour in the fish house. At the time I was frustrated with the book and did not want to work on it anymore. I just wanted to fish. We happened to tune in a broadcast from a station in Chicago. Do you know what the sermon was about? That's right—Jonah.

I started to get the hint and got back to work on the book when I got home. After all, somewhere in the writing process I had added Jonah references to the novel itself because the main character's story parallels that of the prophet. He is also apathetic about the possible fulfillment of prophecy using the technology he helped create. It was an apt analogy, more or less.

In my own life, the references occurred so frequently that I started writing down their dates and how they happened. The references did not stop until I finished the fourth version of the manuscript. What becomes of the book from here is not up to me anymore. God taught me a valuable lesson in obedience and He proved that if He gives you a task, He will help you see it through. Additionally, the biggest critic throughout the writing process was not found in an external source—it was me.

The point of all of this is that an artist of faith needs to "check in" with God on a regular basis but not just for inspiration and strength. An artist also needs to give thanks for the gifts and the ability to serve. As Paul wrote in Philippians 4:6 – 7, "Be careful for nothing; but in every thing by prayer and supplication with thanksgiving let your requests be made known unto God. And the peace of God, which passeth all understanding, shall keep your hearts and minds through Christ Jesus."

- 10 -

The Great Mystery Writer

"It is the glory of God to conceal a thing: but the honour of kings is to search out a matter." – Proverbs 25:2

Sometimes a little mystery is a good thing. It can be inspirational when it comes to creating art. Scripture, too, has multiple instances where not everything is explained from God's perspective. Beside unfulfilled prophecy, there are several situations where God purposely spoke in parables or riddles. Parables appear in the Old Testament in a few places, most notably in Ezekiel chapters 17 and 24, and in Psalms 49 and 78. Jesus, of course, spoke 37 parables (or 39, depending on how they are counted) in the New Testament which confused his disciples at first. Why did He do that?

In Matthew 13:10, the disciples asked the same question. "Why speakest thou unto them in parables?" Jesus replied, "Because it is given unto you to know the mysteries of the kingdom of heaven, but to them it is not given. For whosoever hath, to him shall be given, and he shall have more abundance: but whosoever hath not, from him shall be taken away even that he hath. Therefore speak I to them in parables: because they seeing see not; and hearing they hear not, neither do they understand." (Matthew 13:11 – 13) Jesus was calling back to Isaiah's commission from God in Isaiah 6:8 – 9. It is not that God wanted no one to understand, it is that the people in Isaiah's time had already begun to harden their hearts towards the Lord. The same was true during Jesus' time.

In addition to parables, the Bible contains mysteries of another variety. Although the Bible lists many "song lyrics" (The Book of

Psalms and elsewhere) we do not know what these lyrics sounded like once they were set to music. One of the earliest recorded songs is found in the Book of Exodus, just after the Israelites crossed the Red Sea and Pharaoh's army was swept away. Often called the "Song of the Sea" (and sometimes a Song of Moses), it runs from Exodus 15:1 – 18 and is followed by a responsive song called the "Song of Miriam" in verses 20 – 21. Both the initial song and the response are similar, with Exodus 15:1 stating, "I will sing unto the Lord, for He hath triumphed gloriously: the horse and his rider hath He thrown into the sea."

Another Song of Moses is found in Deuteronomy 31:30 – 32:43 and was written at the end of his life. The subject of this particular one is different and in sharp contrast to the one given at the Red Sea crossing. Here, God instructed Moses just before his death that the Israelites will eventually rebel despite taking the Promised Land under Joshua. In Deuteronomy 31:19, God said, "Now therefore write ye this song for you, and teach it the children of Israel: put it in their mouths, that this song may be a witness for Me against the children of Israel." Moses then announced the song and was buried a short time later on Mount Nebo.

Interestingly enough, the Song of Moses appears again in the Book of Revelation, coupled with another song, being sung by believers who gain victory over the Beast and stand on a sea of glass holding harps of God (Revelation 15:2). It reads, "And they sing the song of Moses the servant of God, and the song of the Lamb, saying, 'Great and marvellous are thy works, Lord God Almighty; just and true are thy ways, thou King of saints.'" (Revelation 15:3) Which song of Moses will it be? Will it be the one sung at the Red Sea or the one given before his death? Most likely it would be the first one, or perhaps it will be a new song altogether.

Some other examples of songs with unknown tunes include the Song of Salvation (Isaiah 26:1 – 6), The Song of the Bow (2 Samuel 1:17 – 27), The Song of Mary (Luke 1:46 – 56), The Song of Solomon, and the Song of Deborah and Barak (Judges 5:1 – 31). The Book of Lamentations, written by the prophet Jeremiah, was composed of several dirges or laments. Often the Book of Lamentations is recited by Jews on Tisha b'Av and is sometimes used during Lent in Christian churches.

Several psalms also have "tunes" listed in their superscriptions but again, nobody knows what these songs sounded like. Psalm 9 refers to a tune called "Death of the Son" and Psalm 22 refers to a tune called "Deer of the Dawn". The KJV states Psalm 45 is called "A Song of Loves" and set to the tune of "The Lillies" (NKJV). Psalm 56 is set to "The Silent Dove in Distant Lands" (NKJV) and Psalm 88 is set to "Mahalath Leannoth". One particular tune is used repeatedly, "Do Not Destroy" (NKJV), in Psalms 57, 58, 59, and 75.

Like the lost tunes of these verses, there are also books in the Bible that are referenced but the content of those books is mostly unknown. 1 Chronicles 29:29 and 2 Chronicles 9:29 reference a "Book of Nathan the Prophet" and 1 Chronicles 29:29 also references a "Book of Gad the Seer". 2 Chronicles 9:29 also mentions a book called "Visions of Iddo the Seer". References to the "Book of Jasher" exist in Joshua 10:13 and 2 Samuel 1:18. There is even a "Book of the Wars of the Lord" found in Numbers 21:14 – 15.

Lastly, there is also a potential "lost epistle" of Paul. Although some forgeries have been created over the years, this letter, if that is what Paul referenced, has been lost. It appears in Colossians 4:16, which reads, "And when this epistle is read among you, cause that it be read also in the church of the Laodiceans; and that ye likewise read the epistle from Laodicea." Nothing is known about the contents of this epistle beyond this verse and some contend it was instead one of his other well-known letters.

Besides these historical songs, books, and the potential missing epistle, several verses in Scripture also refer to a book called the "Book of Life" or the "Lamb's Book of Life". It is referenced six times in the Book of Revelation and may also be the same as the "Book of the Living" found in Psalm 69:28. It is unclear if these are connected to the "Book of Remembrance" found in Malachi 3:16 which reads, "Then they that feared the Lord spake often one to another: and the Lord hearkened, and heard it, and a book of remembrance was written before Him for them that feared the Lord, and that thought upon His name." It is also unclear if there is any connection to the book listed in Psalm 56. Verse eight of that psalm reads, "Thou tellest my wanderings: put thou my tears into thy bottle: are they not in thy book?"

In the Book of Revelation, the Book of Life is described as

containing a list of those who have overcome and are able to enter into the New Jerusalem. It will also be used at the Final Judgment (Revelation 3:5, 20:12, 21:27). Those whose names are not written in the book, if they are alive during the End Times, will worship the First Beast as described in Revelation 13:1 – 10. This is also mentioned in Revelation 17:8. Revelation 20:15 offers this stark warning, "And whosoever was not found written in the book of life was cast into the lake of fire." Revelation 20:12 also describes other books that will be used in the judgment process, stating, "And I saw the dead, small and great, stand before God; and the books were opened: and another book was opened, which is the book of life: and the dead were judged out of those things which were written in the books, according to their works."

How then does one get their name listed in the "Book of Life"? The answer is found in John 3:16 – 17 which states, "For God so loved the world, that He gave His only begotten Son, that whosoever believeth in Him should not perish, but have everlasting life. For God sent not His Son into the world to condemn the world; but that the world through Him might be saved."

Then there was the mysterious scene where Jesus wrote in the sand in front of the scribes and the Pharisees. In John 8:3 – 11, the scribes and the Pharisees brought an adulterous woman before Jesus. They asked Him, "Master, this woman was taken in adultery, in the very act. Now Moses in the law commanded us, that such should be stoned: but what sayest thou?" (verses 4 – 5) They tried to tempt him, but His only reply was an action. "But Jesus stooped down, and with His finger wrote on the ground, as though He heard them not." (verse six)

They continued to pester Him, and He "lifted up himself, and said unto them, 'He that is without sin among you, let him first cast a stone at her.' And again he stooped down, and wrote on the ground." (verses 7 – 8) Eventually they all left and Jesus asked the woman, "Where are those thine accusers? Hath no man condemned thee?" (verse 10) She replied, "No man, Lord," to which He replied, "Neither do I condemn thee: go, and sin no more." (verse 11) Although this section of Scripture is somewhat in dispute (in does not exist in some versions of the earliest manuscripts), it is apparent that Jesus wrote something that the scribes and the Pharisees could not counter. What did He write? One can only speculate, but it subtly calls back to how God wrote the Ten Commandments down for Moses using His finger.

In closing, the apostle John made an intriguing comment at the end of his gospel. In John 21:15 it reads, "And there are also many other things which Jesus did, the which, if they should be written every one, I suppose that even the world itself could not contain the books that should be written." In essence, there were innumerable other things that Jesus did that were *not* recorded in the Gospels. As it turns out, it really did not matter because in John 20:30 – 31 he wrote, "And many other signs truly did Jesus in the presence of His disciples, which are not written in this book: but these are written, that ye might believe that Jesus is the Christ, the Son of God; and that believing ye might have life through His name." What John is saying is that even if more signs and actions were recorded it would be irrelevant because ultimately comes down to an act of faith.

Perhaps the biggest mystery is the nature of the Bible itself. It has endless depth or as Paul wrote in Romans 11:33, "O the depth of the riches both of the wisdom and knowledge of God! How unsearchable are His judgments, and His ways past finding out!" What makes it more intriguing is that one can remove parts of the Bible but the message remains intact. In fact, if you dig enough, you will find the Gospel is buried all throughout the Old Testament in the form of grace, appearances by Jesus, and manifestations of the Holy Spirit.

Jesus also taught two disciples about Himself on the road to Emmaus (Luke 24:13 – 35) using what was essentially the Old Testament. In Luke 24:27 we read, "And beginning at Moses and all the prophets, He expounded unto them in all the scriptures the things concerning Himself." Why didn't anybody before Him put all the pieces together? Some elements of prophecy were purposely hidden until the right moment. Additionally, like any great mystery, sometimes that is a role best left to the Author Himself. After all, in Hebrews 12:2 it reads that we need to look to Jesus as "the author and finisher of our faith; who for the joy that was set before Him endured the cross, despising the shame, and is set down at the right hand of the throne of God."

Bibliography

Card, Michael. *Scribbling in the Sand.* Downers Grove: InterVarsity Press, 2002.

Hays, J. Daniel. *The Temple and the Tabernacle: A Study of God's Dwelling Places from Genesis to Revelation.* Grand Rapids: Baker Books, 2016.

Maier, Paul L. *Josephus: The Essential Works.* Grand Rapids: Kregel Publications, 1994.

Schaeffer, Francis A. *Art and the Bible.* Downers Grove: InterVarsity Press, 1973.

Tenney, Merrill C. and Silva, Moises, editors. *The Zondervan Encyclopedia of the Bible*, Volumes 1-5. Grand Rapids: Zondervan, 2009.

About the Author

Michael Galloway is an outdoors enthusiast whose interests include camping, fishing, hiking, writing, and technology. He has a degree in Journalism, and has been writing software in one language or another for over twenty years. He currently lives in Minnesota with his family.

* * *

Also by Michael Galloway

An Echo Through the Trees
Theft at the Speed of Light
Horizons
Gathering the Wind
Corridors
Fractal Standard Time
Ionotatron
Chronopticus Rising
The Chronopticus Chronicles Series
Race the Sky
The Hammer of Amalynth
Windows Out
The Fire and the Anvil

Made in the USA
San Bernardino, CA
03 June 2020